EXPLORING THE UNSEARCHABLE RICHES OF CHRIST

Dedication

To my precious wife who has been
my constant companion, my kindest
critic and my faithful co-laborer these
many years, and who also shares with me
the "Blessed Hope."

To her I gratefully dedicate this book.

EXPLORING THE UNSEARCHABLE RICHES OF CHRIST

The Key that Unlocks the Word, Rightly Divided

By

Paul M. Sadler

President, BEREAN BIBLE SOCIETY
Editor, BEREAN SEARCHLIGHT
Radio Teacher, BIBLE TIME
Author, THE TRIUMPH OF HIS GRACE
(Preparing Ourselves For the Rapture)
And other Bible Studies

BEREAN BIBLE SOCIETY
N112 W17761 Mequon Rd.
Germantown, Wisconsin 53022
(Metro Milwaukee)

Copyright, 1993

by

BEREAN BIBLE SOCIETY
N112 W17761 Mequon Rd.
Germantown, Wisconsin 53022
(Metro Milwaukee)

Third Printing

Library of Congress Cataloging in Publication Data
Sadler, Paul M.
Exploring the Unsearchable Riches of Christ: an exegesis on the Word of God, rightly divided.

Includes bibliographical references and index.
ISBN 0-9644541-0-6
1. Bible. 2. Grace (Theology). 3. Biblical Teaching. 4. Title.

All rights reserved. No part of this book may be reproduced in any form without permission in writing, except in the case of brief quotations in critical articles or reviews.

All Scripture quotations in this book are from *"The Old Scofield Reference Bible"* 1909, 1917, 1937, 1945 by Oxford University Press, Inc.   King James Version

Printed in the United States of America
Worzalla Publishing Co.   Stevens Point, Wisconsin

CONTENTS

In Grateful Appreciation 7

Preface 9

Introduction 11

1. **Rightly Dividing the Word of Truth**
   Rightly Dividing the Word • Where Did the Old Testament Begin? • The New Testament • In Summary 15

2. **God's Major Division in His Word**
   The Two Programs of God • The Prophetic Program • The Mystery • A Closing Word 25

3. **The Apostleship and Message of St. Paul**
   Who Chose Paul? • Paul and Matthias • Paul Is Not the Thirteenth Apostle • Paul's Unique Message • Why Did Paul Go to the Jew First? • The Stoning of Stephen • To the Jew First • Paul's Three Pronouncements 35

4. **Dispensationalism**
   Distinguishing Between the Ages and Dispensations • Correlating the Ages and the Dispensations • Further Clarification on the Eternal State • Appointment With Destiny • Deliverance • A Closing Thought • Dispensational Graph 51

5. **Characteristics of the Mystery**
   The Secret • A Controversial Passage • Other Mysteries • The Mystery and the Volume of the Book • A Supplementary Word 72

6. **The Two Ministries of Christ**
   Christ's Earthly Ministry • The Heavenly Ministry of Christ • An Enlightening Contrast • Chart 82

5

7. **The Body of Christ**
   A Distinction That Matters • Being in Christ • In
   Christ Redemptively • Peter's Helping Hand •
   Dispensationally in Christ 91

8. **The One Spirit**
   The Comforter • The Kingdom Gospel and the Spirit •
   The Mystery and the Spirit • Results of the Spirit-
   Centered Life • In Closing 106

9. **Identifying Our One Hope**
   Defining the Biblical Word "Hope" • In Search of Our
   Hope • Hope of Salvation • The Hope of Resurrection •
   Paul, Our Pattern 117

10. **One Lord**
    A Divine Illustration • The Headship of Christ •
    Christ's Authority Over All 127

11. **One Faith**
    The Ministry of Reconciliation • Imputation •
    Ambassadors For Christ 136

12. **One Baptism**
    The Purpose of Water Baptism • A New Administration
    • Identification 144

13. **One God**
    The Fatherhood of God • A Pauline View of God • The
    Temple of God 154

14. **Our Blessed Hope**
    Words of Comfort • The Secret Coming of Christ •
    The Objective of the Rapture 163

15. **Practical Instructions for Living Under Grace**
    Seeking Things Above • Setting Our Affection
    On Things Above 173

Scripture Index 179

IN GRATEFUL APPRECIATION

To my family who was more than understanding and patient during the many hours I spent nestled away in my study writing. Their patience will surely be rewarded in that day the Lord appears.

To my beloved wife, Vicki, who originally gave me the idea for the book and encouraged me to take on the challenge. She was also responsible for the painstaking task of typing the original manuscript. The Scripture index that appears in the back of this volume is to be attributed to her as well.

To my co-laborer, Richard Hunt, who laid out and typeset the entire manuscript. He had the *patience of Job* as numerous corrections and adjustments had to be made along the way. Dick is a "beloved brother" in the truest sense of the word.

Heartfelt thanks to our dear Brother Fred Wisniewski, who faithfully proofread the manuscript and offered a number of insightful suggestions, many of which were implemented by the author. Special thanks to Pastors Ivan Burgener, David Caslander and Dennis Kiszonas who were kind enough to critique Chapter four.

The photograph of *Glacier Bay* in Alaska which graces the front jacket is by Uniphoto Picture Agency, Washington, D. C.

Finally, thanks be unto God for supplying the opportunity and the strength to complete this work. It is the author's earnest prayer that God will be *glorified* in this labor of love.
—The Author

PREFACE

Charles Dickens statement, "It was the best of times; it was the worst of times," epitomizes the era leading up to the impartation of God's *secret purpose,* which had been hidden from ages and generations past. On one hand this period witnessed some of the cruelest injustices this world has ever known, while on the other hand it gave birth to a *new* divine revelation.

This volume explores the *Unsearchable Riches of Christ* which were originally dispensed to the Apostle Paul. Inasmuch as the rediscovery of this truth has only been since the Reformation it has generated a swarm of critics. While it is true that the *message of God's grace* has been a lost jewel for many centuries, this teaching has always been the very soul of the Pauline epistles.

The reason that the *Mystery* was obscure for so many generations was due in part to the failure of the Church to recognize the distinctive apostleship and message of St. Paul. These seeds of discontent were already being sown back in the apostle's day, for he wrote to Timothy: "This thou knowest, that all they which are in Asia be turned away from me; of whom are Phygellus and Hermogenes." To turn from Paul, as "all in Asia" had done was to reject his *God-given* revelation, which he had received from the Lord of glory (II Tim. 1:15; I Cor. 14:37). This, of course, brought the swift judgment of God, which plunged Christendom into the Dark Ages. Sadly, tradition reigned supreme during this period, resulting in the spiritual bondage of countless souls.

It was not until the dawn of the Protestant Reformation that God in His infinite mercy began to allow the recovery of this message, which once had so blessed the early Church. Thus, Martin Luther shook Europe when he saw the great Pauline truth—"The just shall live by faith." During this heroic time importance was once again placed on Paul's revelation, which is clearly witnessed in the flight of the French Huguenots. With the forces of organized religion preparing to persecute them, they fled out of harm's way, but not before tearing Paul's epistles from their Bibles to take with them on their journey.

The Huguenots were followed by devout men of God such as J. N. Darby, who is credited with the recovery of the *pretribulational Rapture.* C. I. Scofield built upon this by uncovering the *dispensational approach* to studying the Scriptures. Others, of course, had preceded him in this Biblical system of interpretation, but Dr. Scofield was the first to plainly differentiate between *Law* and *Grace.* Later, God raised up Pastor J. C. O'Hair who took a giant step in emphasizing the need to *rightly divide the Word of truth.* He was instrumental in showing the Church the necessity of distinguishing between *Prophecy* and the *Mystery.* Finally, Pastor C. R. Stam, who was a contemporary of Mr. O'Hair, shed even further light on Paul's gospel as he ably defended *the faith* in his writings.

We owe a great debt of gratitude to those who, in the face of almost unbelievable opposition, have retrieved for us the *gospel of the grace of God.* Today, then, we bear a tremendous responsibility to "make all men see what is the fellowship of the Mystery." May God help us to stand uncompromisingly for this wonderful truth, lest the Church again lose sight of it.

INTRODUCTION

There are two questions frequently asked by those who are pondering the validity of the *Grace Message*. First, if our position is true, then why has the Church largely failed to see it? Secondly, why doesn't the Grace Movement have large numbers, if this is truly God's message for today?

These are indeed legitimate questions that deserve thoughtful consideration. There are numerous reasons as to why believers have been so reluctant to acknowledge Paul's gospel. *Tradition* ranks high on the list. Many are satisfied to simply attend church every Sunday and accept what is being taught without ever searching the Scriptures for themselves. In defense of their church tradition we often hear: "If it was good enough for my grandfather and my father, it's good enough for me!"

Fear runs a close second to tradition. Sometime ago we heard from a Godly father who had given a set of our books to his son, who was a pastor of a large denominational assembly out west. Lo and behold, if the son didn't come to rejoice in the *Mystery!* When his father inquired as to when he was going to preach it, the son replied, "I can't, Dad—the church would never accept it." When positions, salaries and retirement plans are at stake the truth many times is swept aside.

Even many of the well-known Fundamentalist leaders of the past, some of whom we have good reason to believe knew about the Mystery, were *silent* because of the fear of men. In fact, it is amazing when reading their writings how they followed one another through the labyrinth of

God's now dormant Prophetic program, leaving their hearers both past and present destitute of the *Unsearchable Riches of Christ*. But they forgot one thing in their haste to remain accepted by the mainstream of Christendom—the Judgment Seat of Christ, where every man will give an account of himself.

In the meantime there are multitudes who have never even heard about the *Mystery*. And the sad part about this is, many of these dear saints sense that something is missing in their understanding of the Scriptures. They are diligently searching for the *key* that unlocks the Word, rightly divided, which is the very subject of this writing.

As to the need to have large numbers as an indication of God's blessing, we have found just the opposite to be the case in the Word of God. When Noah and his family disembarked from the Ark, only 8 souls carried the truth into the new world. Moving down the corridor of time to the days of Gideon, out of an army of 32,000 God chose a mere 300 from the camp in Israel to conquer the Midianites. Literally hundreds of thousands were saved under our Lord's earthly ministry; however, only 120 deemed it necessary to obey His command to tarry at Jerusalem to await the arrival of the Holy Spirit. Those who have been willing to stand for the truth have always been in the *minority* in every generation, and today is no exception.

The chapters that follow are the fruits of preaching the gospel of the grace of God over a period of nearly twenty-five years. Therefore, it is the author's desire that our faith rest in the living Word of God and not in the commandments of men!

Sir Winston Churchill told a wartime Parliament, "I have nothing to offer but blood, toil, tears and sweat." His vivid words stirred a nation to action. Likewise, we trust this volume will stir your heart anew to stand with us in defense of Paul's gospel. With God's help and with the truth on our side we shall be more than conquerors!

—Pastor Paul M. Sadler

Chicago, Illinois
November 12, 1992

1
Rightly Dividing the Word of Truth

"Study to show thyself approved unto God, a workman that needeth not to be ashamed, rightly dividing the Word of truth."

—*II Timothy 2:15*

The purpose of this study is to establish the reader in God's message for the Church, the Body of Christ, during this present age of Grace. The content of this volume has been developed over nearly a twenty-five year period and we pray it may help you enjoy the Word of God in a deeper sense. It clearly transformed this author's life when he first came to a knowledge of the Word, rightly divided. Before that time, the Bible was a closed book which seemed to generate more questions than answers. But thanks be unto God, we can add our voice to many of the past and present, that the key which *unlocks* the sacred secret is *rightly dividing the Word of truth.*

Perhaps for some we are about to embark upon a journey through uncharted waters. However, we will soon show that the Apostle Paul charted the way many years before us. While the Church at large has lost its course on the *Sea of Confusion,* the *light* of the glorious gospel of grace will safely *guide* all those who seek the truth to a clearer knowledge of God's will. As we begin our journey together, we request that the reader set aside any preconceived ideas which may prove to be a hindrance. Our faith must rest squarely on what God has revealed; therefore, it is our earnest desire that the reader be a Berean and study whether these things are so (Acts 17:11).

RIGHTLY DIVIDING THE WORD

The Holy Spirit places great importance upon the need to properly divide the Word of truth. Our Lord Himself rightly divided the Scriptures when He entered the synagogue in Nazareth where He read from the Book of Isaiah:

> "The Spirit of the Lord is upon me, because he hath anointed me to preach the gospel to the poor; he hath sent me to heal the brokenhearted, to preach deliverance to the captives, and recovering of sight to the blind, to set at liberty them that are bruised, to preach the acceptable year of the Lord" (Isa. 61:1,2 cf. Luke 4:16-20).

The Lord abruptly closed the book without reading the remainder of the prophecy which continues, *". . . and the day of vengeance of our God; to comfort all that mourn. . . ."* Of course, this was done intentionally, because the first part of this prophecy was *fulfilled* before the very eyes of His hearers (Luke 4:21). However, this could not be said of the latter part, which predicts the vengeance of God during the future tribulation period and the millennial *comfort* to follow.

The following statement may be shocking to some, but it is true: "Our God is a God of *division!*" In the beginning, He divided the waters which were under the firmament from the waters which were above the firmament (Gen. 1:7). God *divided* the waters upon the earth, thus allowing the dry land to appear (Gen. 1:9,10). On the fourth day of creation He *divided* the day from the night (Gen. 1:14). God also instructs us that His Word must be *rightly divided* if we ever hope to understand the counsel of His will.

The first question one is led to ask in this connection is: Where has God placed the *major division* in His Word? Church tradition declares that it is between the Old and the New Testament. Almost no one questions that the Old Testament begins with Genesis and ends with Malachi and was written to the *nation Israel;* or that the New Testament, Matthew through the Book of Revelation is addressed to the *Church, the Body of Christ.* Quite honestly, we believe it is time that this traditional view be challenged on the basis of its Scriptural inaccuracy. Like sheep following one another down the wrong path, the Church has fallen victim to the same.

It is difficult to determine who first introduced the format commonly known as the Old and New Testaments. One thing we certainly know, it is a man-made division. Whoever was responsible, undoubtedly, surmised that since there was a 400 year period between Malachi and Matthew, known as the Intertestament period, this was the logical place to *mark* the major division in God's Word. We believe that this theory, though seemingly conclusive, has pointed one of the most important guideposts in the Word of God in the wrong direction, and has caused untold confusion down through the centuries.

WHERE DID THE OLD TESTAMENT BEGIN?

"Now therefore, if ye will obey my voice indeed, and keep my Covenant, then ye shall be a peculiar treasure unto me above all people: for all the earth is mine: And ye shall be unto me a kingdom of priests, and an holy nation. These are the words which thou shalt speak unto the children of Israel" (Ex. 19:5,6).

The first reference in our Bibles to the *Old Testament* is found here in Exodus 19:5. This means that well over 2500 years had elapsed before God *gave* the Law to Israel. Of course, the Covenant or Testament oftentimes referred to as the Law was *conditional*. In other words, *if* Israel complied with all 613 commandments and ordinances God would bless her and make her His peculiar people. Over the course of time one thing became evident: The Law was *not* given to save. Rather it was to give her a knowledge of sin (Rom. 3:19,20). God's chosen nation soon became thankful for the sacrificial system whereby they could receive the atonement of their sins.

Exodus chapters 19-23 are only the preliminary ground work leading up to the actual *inauguration* of the Old Testament. Technically speaking, the Law was not *binding* upon the people until it was initiated by the shedding of blood. *All* of God's Covenants are established by blood. Please consider the following passage:

> "And Moses took half of the blood, and put it in basins; and half of the blood he sprinkled on the altar. And he took the book of the Covenant, and read in the audience of the people: and they said, All that the Lord hath said will we do, and be obedient. And Moses took the blood, and sprinkled it on the people, and said, Behold the blood of the Covenant, which the Lord hath made with you concerning all these words" (Ex. 24:6-8).

So then, if the Old Testament did not begin until

Exodus 24, to *whom* was the Book of Genesis written? The answer to this question is but one example of the inconsistencies in the traditional view held by the vast majority of believers. But there is even a more pressing question that deserves our most thoughtful attention. When was the Covenant of the Law *terminated* by God? As mentioned earlier, most hold that the Old Testament ended when Malachi closed the book that bears his name and said, AMEN!! Here again we must inquire: What saith the Scriptures?

> "But when the fulness of the time was come, God sent forth His Son, made of a woman, made under the Law, To redeem them that were under the Law. . ." (Gal. 4:4,5).

Under the supervision of the Holy Spirit the Apostle Paul reveals, by means of inspiration, that our Lord Jesus Christ during His years upon this earth lived *under the Old Testament*. In fact, the primary purpose of Christ's first coming was to redeem those who spent their lifetime in bondage to the Law of Moses. Turning back to the earthly ministry of Christ for a moment, we have selected *three* Scripture verses from the gospel according to Matthew to substantiate the above conclusion.

> "Think not that I am come to destroy the Law, or the prophets: I am not come to destroy, but to fulfill" (Matt. 5:17).

This passage implies that there were those in the time of Christ who called His motives into question. If the pious Pharisees had not asked it, they were surely thinking to themselves—The institution of the Law of Moses has stood for over 1500 years, so why is this man who claims to be sent from God, now going to destroy it? Our

Lord quickly disarmed His critics and in so doing teaches us that one of His missions was to fulfill the Law, which plainly indicates He *observed* it to the letter.

Leprosy was a dreadful disease in Biblical times that struck fear in the heart. According to the Law, the leper was never permitted to enter the camp of Israel without first being pronounced clean by the priest (Lev. 4:1-7). Leper colonies were avoided like the plague, but in the event someone came into contact with a leper they often cried aloud, "leper, leper, leper!" which was humiliating to say the least. Our Lord, on the other hand, had compassion on these poor souls; thus, on more than one occasion He healed their infirmity. One such case is found in Matt. 8:3,4:

> "And Jesus put forth His hand, and touched Him, saying, I will; be thou clean. And immediately his leprosy was cleansed. And Jesus saith unto him, See thou tell no man; but go thy way, show thyself to the priest, and offer the gift that Moses commanded, for a testimony unto them."

The diligent reader will agree that the Old Testament was still *alive and well* up to this point as our Lord tells the leper to show himself unto the priest. This teaches us that not only did Christ live in perfect obedience to the Law, He *required* that others do the same as well.

Our third passage is found in Matthew 23:1-3 where our Lord, who is now standing in the shadow of the Cross, utters these solemn words of warning:

> "Then spake Jesus to the multitude, and to His disciples, saying, The scribes and the Pharisees sit in Moses' seat: All therefore whatsoever they bid you

observe, that observe and do; but do not ye after their works: for they say, and do not."

Need we say more? We believe it can be correctly said that *Matthew, Mark, Luke* and *John* are Old Testament Scriptures. This may not set well with some; nevertheless, it is the true testimony of Holy Scripture.

According to Colossians 2:14 the *abolition* of the Law took place the day Christ died. On the divine side of the ledger, full payment for the debt of our sins was made at Calvary. However, on the human side, the actual *record* that payment was made in full was to be manifested in due time through Paul's gospel (I Tim. 2:3-7). Furthermore, this explains why the Law continued to be observed after the Cross, although we know it gradually lost its mastery through the revelation given to Paul who affirmed that the Law was done away that *"grace might reign"* (Rom. 6:14). Philip Bliss' hymn *Once for All* conveys the thought beautifully: "Free from the Law—O happy condition! Jesus hath bled and there is remission; Cursed by the Law and bruised by the fall, Grace hath redeemed us once for all!"

THE NEW TESTAMENT

"And he took bread, and gave thanks, and brake it, and gave unto them, saying, This is My body which is given for you: this do in remembrance of Me. Likewise also the cup after supper, saying, This cup is the New Testament in My blood, which is shed for you" (Luke 22:19,20).

Contrary to popular belief, the New Testament did not begin in Matthew, chapter one with the birth of Christ. Actually, it was as our Lord was about to face His greatest trial at the Cross that He said to His disciples in the upper room, "*This is the New Testament in my blood.*"

It is important for the reader to distinguish here in Luke's gospel between the *Last Supper* and the *Lord's Supper.*[1] The Passover meal, commonly called the *Last Supper,* was celebrated first. Moreover, this was one final act our Lord performed in fulfilling the righteousness of the Old Testament before the introduction of the New.

Strictly regulated by the Law, the Passover was to be observed in the following manner: First, the Passover lamb must be without spot or blemish. Next, the lamb's blood was to be shed, although *no bone* in its body was to be broken. The Israelites also were required to eat unleavened bread at this meal, which symbolized their need to be *free* from sin that they might glorify God. The bitter herbs reminded the Hebrews of the bitter bondage their forefathers experienced in the land of Egypt. The

---

1. According to I Corinthians 11:23 the Apostle Paul received a *special* revelation concerning the *Lord's Supper;* therefore we believe it is to be celebrated today without reservation. It is easy to see, of course, how the subject of the Lord's Supper can sometimes be confusing, since the Church has taught that it is one of the last two remaining ordinances. But what saith the Scriptures? Christ has blotted ". . . out the handwriting of ordinances that was against us, which was contrary to us, and took it out of the way. . ." (Col. 2:14). The testimony of Holy Scripture declares that there are *no* ordinances to be observed during the dispensation of Grace.

It should be remembered however, that the Lord's Supper was never, nor will it ever be, an ordinance. The Spirit of God makes it explicitly clear that it is a *memorial.* As Paul says concerning the elements, it is to be done "in remembrance of me [Christ]." The *Lincoln Memorial* in Washington D.C., is a solemn reminder that it was President Lincoln who signed the Emancipation Proclamation to free the slaves. In like manner, when we clutch that morsel of bread in our hand and partake of the cup of blessing, it *reminds* us that Christ died to free us from the bondage of our sins.

Passover feast looked forward to the day when Israel will be finally and forever delivered from both her physical and spiritual bondage, the fulfillment of which was made possible by the sacrificial death of Christ (Luke 1:67-77; John 19:31-33; I Cor. 5:7).

As the Passover meal was drawing to a close and after Judas had left the room, the Master instituted what has come to be known as the *Lord's Supper* (Matt. 26:17-28). Undoubtedly, this was done purposely to show that the unbeliever should never have a part in this holy observance. Also, our Lord had chosen this hour to introduce the New Testament, foretold by the prophets of old. The House of Israel was exclusively given the promise of the New Covenant, which incidentally contains *all* spiritual blessings. Please read prayerfully the words of Jeremiah the prophet:

> "Behold, the days come, saith the Lord, that I will make a New Covenant with the House of Israel, and with the House of Judah" (Jer. 31:31).

Some of the New Testament blessings that Israel[2] will ultimately realize in the future millennial kingdom are: God *will* forgive her sins on the basis of Christ's shed blood (Matt. 26:28). In that day He *will* also give believing Israel a new heart and *cause* her to be indwelt by the Holy Spirit (Ezek. 36:26,27). The New Testament is therefore an *unconditional* Covenant in which God *will* empower His chosen people to willingly obey what was required of them under the Old Covenant (Jer. 31:33).

As we shall see, even though the New Covenant was

---

2. We thus conclude that Israel is the New Testament Church.

never promised to the Gentiles, we have received the blessings of it by *grace*. This conclusion is based on Romans 15:27: "For if the Gentiles have been made partakers of their [Israel's] spiritual things, their duty is also to minister unto them in carnal things." Hence, the apostle informs us that we too are able ministers of the New Testament (II Cor. 3:6). The importance of this cannot be overstated for this reason—Christ has shed His precious blood *once for all* in direct accordance with this Covenant. If we have no connection to it, then Christ must return to die again for the Gentiles, which is *unthinkable* (Heb. 10:9,10).

IN SUMMARY

Perhaps the following outline will shed further light on the foregoing thoughts:

Old Testament	New Testament
Given to the nation Israel (Ex. 19:5)	Made with the House of Israel. (Jer. 31:31)
A. Conditional Covenant	A. Unconditional Covenant (except for faith)

B. 613 Commandments
  1. Moral Law
  2. Civil Law
  3. Ceremonial Law
	B. Spiritual Promises
	  1. Cleansing with blood
	  2. A new heart
	  3. The Holy Spirit

C. Duration 1500 years— from Moses to the Cross.	C. Duration 1000 years.—The kingdom through eternity.

If both the Old and the New Testaments were established with the House of Israel, then this could not possibly be the major division in God's Word, which raises the question, *Where do we fit into the picture as members of the Church, the Body of Christ?*

2
God's Major Division in His Word

"In the beginning God created the heaven and the earth."

—*Genesis 1:1*

The Protestant Reformation produced a number of giants in the faith, among whom was Miles Coverdale, who gave us these practical instructions for studying the Word of God:

"It shall greatly help ye to understand Scripture if thou mark not only what is spoken or written, but of whom and to whom, with what words, at what time, where, to what intent, with what circumstances, considering what goeth before and what followeth after."

In other words, while all of the Bible is for us, it is not all written directly to us. For example, in the Old Testament God commanded His people that they were to observe the law of the sabbath. On the seventh day (Saturday) of each week those under this regulation were *not permitted* to buy or sell, gather sticks, kindle a fire, prepare a meal, do any type of work or journey much more than a mile (Ex. 31:12-17; 35:3). Those who dared to violate this holy ordinance were to suffer the death penalty. Thus, the sabbath was to be a day of physical rest, which foreshadowed the *rest* Israel will enjoy in the millennium.

Forgive me, but I must ask: Are you observing the sabbath as commanded in the Word of God? Needless to say, the answer is rather obvious. This illustration, though, does make the very valid point that *not all Scripture is written directly to us.* It is essential that the reader acknowledge that there has been a significant *change* from one divine program to another. In our first chapter we established the fact that while the Old and New Testaments affect us, they were not made with the Gentiles, nor do they constitute God's major division in His Word. Where then has God placed the major division in His Word?

THE TWO PROGRAMS OF GOD

It is noteworthy that God said He "... created the heaven and the earth," when He could have simply said that He created the *world.* Unlike man, however, God does not use words frivolously. He is meticulous in His choice of words and for good reason—many times it is to convey two thoughts in one. Such is the case here; God would have us understand that He is the Creator of heaven and the Creator of earth, which strongly implies that He has a different *plan and purpose* for each.

Allow me to illustrate what I mean. Perhaps you have the unique privilege of owning a grand piano. First and foremost, it is a beautiful piece of workmanship that accentuates the furniture in any room. But it also serves a *purpose,* which is to produce music that is gratifying to the ear.

God's program for the earth is identified as *Prophecy,* while His program for the heavenlies is known as the *Mystery.* A program is defined as "... a plan or procedure for dealing with some matter." For instance, we might watch a documentary of American history followed by a documentary on wildlife. Both are programs, but they deal with two entirely different subjects; the same is true with God's Word. The theme of God's Prophetic program embraces *Christ's reign upon the earth* in the future millennial kingdom. On the other hand, the Mystery points to *our exaltation with Christ in the heavenlies.*

Just as the great Continental Divide separates the rivers flowing toward the Atlantic from those flowing toward the Pacific, in like manner the Word of God is divided into two parts—*Prophecy* and *Mystery.* Sad to say, many dear saints have proceeded down the wrong side of the Continental Divide of Holy Scripture. They are peacefully floating down the *Prophetic* river unaware that a dangerous falls lie ahead. Indeed, they will be saved because the Lord cannot deny Himself, but they will suffer terrible *loss* at the Judgment Seat of Christ (I Cor. 3:9-15). Those whose eyes have been open to see the Mystery are proceeding down the proper side of the *divide.* They should be prepared, however, to shoot the rapids, inasmuch as those who stand for the truth of Paul's gospel will face almost unbelievable opposition. Thankfully, these waters flow into an ocean of *eternal reward* at journey's end.

THE PROPHETIC PROGRAM

"For we have not followed cunningly devised fables, when we made known unto you the power and coming of our Lord Jesus Christ, but were eyewitnesses of His majesty. For He received from God the Father honor and glory, when there came such a voice to Him from the excellent glory, This is my beloved Son, in Whom I am well pleased. . . . We have also a more sure word of prophecy; whereunto ye do well that ye take heed. . ." (II Peter 1:16,17,19).

Here Peter recounts the experience he had on the Mount of Transfiguration. Prior to this memorable occasion our Lord taught the disciples about His impending death at Jerusalem. Aware that they were troubled by this announcement, the Master spoke these words of consolation: *"Verily I say unto you, There be some standing here, which shall not taste of death, till they see the Son of Man coming in His kingdom"* (Matt. 16:28).

On the surface it may appear as though all of the disciples died without ever witnessing the fulfillment of this event. However, we believe our Lord's words were fulfilled to the very letter when He took Peter, James and John to the mount and was transfigured before their very eyes. Accordingly, we are told, "*. . . His face did shine as the sun, and His raiment was white as the light."*

Peter, James and John were given a glimpse of what it will be like when Christ returns to establish His millennial kingdom. Years later Peter tells his hearers that he was an eyewitness of the Lord's coming glory. He also informs those to whom he was writing that he heard the voice of God stating, *"This is my beloved Son, in whom I am well pleased."* In essence Peter was saying, I have had an experience to end all experiences, but don't take my word as the final authority. *"We have also a more sure word of prophecy; whereunto ye do well that ye take heed."* Peter prudently turns his hearers to the Scriptures where these events are foretold by the prophets of old. Jeremiah predicted long ago:

> "Behold, the days come, saith the Lord, that I will raise unto David a righteous Branch, and a King shall reign and prosper, and shall execute judgment and justice in the earth" (Jer. 23:5).

The prophetic saints then were expecting a king to come who would conquer their enemies and set up a kingdom of righteousness upon the earth.

Our forefathers wisely formed our government around the principle of what is known as the *separation of powers*. They divided the authority among three branches: executive, legislative and judicial. This means that a legislator cannot hold the office of the president during the same term, thus avoiding a monopoly of power.

For the most part the same was true in Israel concerning the affairs of God. A king, for example, was never permitted to hold the office of a priest and vice versa. Those who attempted to usurp the authority of another's office suffered the swift retribution of God (I Sam. 13:8-14). Christ, however, holds all three offices: prophet, priest and king of Israel, for all power and authority is vested in Him. Therefore, He is the one who will rule and reign in righteousness in the kingdom to come.

Some have wrongly concluded that the prophetic saints looked forward to going to heaven to be with the Lord. Quite the contrary: Since the kingdom was to be set up upon the earth those who were under this program naturally had an *earthly hope*. The patriarch Job gives us the most ancient record as to the hope of the saints of his day.

> "For I know that my Redeemer liveth, and that He shall stand at the latter day upon the EARTH: And though after my skin worms destroy this body, yet in my flesh shall I see God" (Job 19:25,26).

Abraham, who was in all probability the contemporary of Job, searched for a city.

"For he looked for a city [on EARTH] which hath foundations, whose builder and maker is God" (Heb. 11:10).

Our Lord lent further credence to this promise when He delivered the Sermon on the Mount.

"Blessed are the meek: for they shall inherit the EARTH" (Matt. 5:5).

Later on in the discourse He taught His disciples to pray accordingly:

"Thy kingdom *come.* Thy will be done in EARTH, as it is in heaven" (Matt. 6:10).

Consequently, those who were saved under this program, such as Abraham, Moses, David, Isaiah, Peter, Stephen and the saved of the future tribulation period all have or had an *earthly hope.*

We should pause here for a moment to address a commonly asked question—If the kingdom is earthly, then why does our Lord frequently refer to it as the *kingdom of heaven?* The answer is twofold: First of all, according to the parable of the nobleman, our Lord is to go into a far country (heaven) to receive for Himself a kingdom, and *return* (Luke 19:11,12). Secondly, when our Lord returns in His Second Coming He will lift the curse from the earth. In that day we are instructed that the desert shall blossom like a rose, the blind shall see, the deaf shall hear again and the lame man shall leap (Isa. 35:1-6). *In short, it will be like heaven on earth!*

One very crucial point which must not be overlooked in this discussion is that the kingdom and earthly reign of Christ has been foretold *since the beginning of the world.*

This is not to say that the saints of old understood every aspect of this unfolding revelation. But the following Scriptures do bear out that the kingdom has been made known from the beginning of time:

> "Blessed be the Lord God of Israel; for He hath visited and redeemed His people, And hath raised up an horn of salvation for us in the house of His servant David [to fulfill the promise given to David concerning the kingdom—II Sam. 7:16,17]; As He spake by the mouth of His holy prophets, which hath been SINCE THE WORLD BEGAN" (Luke 1:68-70).

> ". . . when the times of refreshing [kingdom] shall come from the presence of the Lord. . . . Whom the heaven must receive until the times of restitution of all things, which God hath spoken by the mouth of all His holy prophets SINCE THE WORLD BEGAN" (Acts 3:19,21).

THE MYSTERY

> "For this cause I Paul, the prisoner of Jesus Christ for you Gentiles, if ye have heard of the dispensation of the grace of God which is given me to you-ward: How that by revelation He made known unto me the Mystery. . ." (Eph. 3:1-3).

The other major program in God's Word is the *Mystery*. Some have concluded that the Mystery is merely the new revelation that Jews and Gentiles are now in one Body. But there is more, far more! When Israel, through whom God was channeling His blessing, rejected her Messiah it brought in an unexpected calamity. God set the wayward nation aside in unbelief. With the stoning of Stephen in Acts 7, the clock of prophecy abruptly stopped, temporarily suspending the Prophetic program.

By all outward appearances this action seemed to leave the world in the depths of despair. But God had a *secret* in mind that He had *not* revealed to the prophets in former dispensations. In His infinite, matchless grace He saved the chief of sinners, Paul, and ushered in a new program called the *Mystery* or the *dispensation of the grace of God.*

The revelation of the Mystery introduces Christ in a completely *new role.* Today He is the Head of the Body, carrying out a *heavenly ministry* on our behalf. Consequently, the Apostle Paul focuses our attention on the *heavenlies,* where Christ is seated at the right hand of God in a position of exaltation. During this age of Grace we do not know Christ as the King of Kings who is prepared to return with the flaming fire of vengeance to execute judgment upon His enemies. Rather we know Him as the God of all grace who has made us sit *together* in heavenly places that we might share in His exaltation (Eph. 1:19-23; 2:6).

Ask the average believer what his or her *hope* is and the response is always the same: Heaven is my home! To be with my Savior who is in heaven! I'm looking forward to being caught up to heaven to forever be with the Lord! But how have these saints come to the conclusion that their hope is heavenly? Surely, it was not through a study of the four gospels, for as we have seen the earthly kingdom is in view in those Scriptures. Amazingly, the hope that many claim today is found *only* in Paul's epistles, even though they have failed to realize that his epistles are the basis of their belief. Paul's revelation abounds with passages that cause us to look heavenward for our consolation.

God's Major Division in His Word

"And hath raised us up together, and made us sit together, in HEAVENLY places in Christ Jesus" (Eph. 2:6).

"For our conversation [citizenship] is in HEAVEN; from whence also we look for the Savior, the Lord Jesus Christ" (Phil. 3:20).

"For the hope which is laid up for you in HEAVEN, whereof ye heard before in the Word of the truth of the gospel" (Col. 1:5).

Since the Holy Spirit marks the beginning of the Body of Christ with the conversion of Paul, all those who have been saved from his conversion to the present have a *heavenly hope*.

One of the outstanding features of the Mystery, unlike the preceding program, is that it was *kept secret* from ages and generations past. Please note carefully the wording of these passages, which convey just the *opposite* of what we found in the former program of prophecy.

"Now to Him that is of power to stablish you according to my gospel, and the preaching of Jesus Christ, according to the revelation of the Mystery, which was KEPT SECRET since the world began" (Rom. 16:25).

"Which in other ages was NOT MADE KNOWN unto the sons of men, as it is now revealed unto His holy apostles and prophets by the Spirit" (Eph. 3:5).

"Even the Mystery which hath been HID from ages and from generations, but now is made manifest to His saints" (Col. 1:26).

We have a challenge for those readers who may be somewhat skeptical of our conclusions, which are taken directly from the Word of God: Although this will be an exercise in futility, try to find the unsearchable (untraceable) riches of Christ in any other writing outside of Paul's epistles. Some of the riches are as follows: The one Body made up of Jews and Gentiles without distinction; our spiritual baptism into Christ's Body; the Rapture of the Church; the Headship of Christ; and we could go on and on.

A CLOSING WORD

Hopefully the following chart will help to reinforce the distinction that God makes between His two programs:

Prophecy	Mystery
1. God's plan and purpose for the earth and Christ's reign upon it. (Kingdom) Matt. 16:28—Matt. 17:1-5—II Peter 1:15-21.	God's plan and purpose for the heavens and our exaltation with Christ in heaven. Eph. 1:19-23; 3:1-4—Col. 3:1-4.
2. Prophetic Saints (Israel) Matt. 10:5,6—Matt. 15:24.	Mystery Saints (Body of Christ) Eph. 1:22,23—I Cor. 12:27.
3. Prophetic Saints have an earthly hope. Job 19:25,26—Gen. 12:1-3—Matt. 5:5.	Body of Christ has a heavenly hope. Eph. 2:6—Col. 1:5—Phil. 3:20.
4. Prophetic Program revealed from the foundation of the world. Luke 1:67-70—Acts 3:21.	Mystery Program was kept secret since the world began. Rom. 16:25—Col. 1:25-27.

The right column is but a sampling of the spiritual blessings we enjoy in Christ. Many others await our further exploration of the Pauline epistles. After we determine what these blessings are, then we are to *set* our affections on things above. This means that we should fill our hearts with them to the point that we desire to know everything there is to know about each and every blessing. Eventually this will filter down to our everyday experience, conforming us more and more to the image of Christ.

3

The Apostleship and Message of St. Paul

> "For I speak to you Gentiles, inasmuch as I am the apostle of the Gentiles, I magnify mine office."
> —*Romans 11:13*

It is an indisputable fact that God has placed the major division in His Word between *Prophecy* and the *Mystery*. As we pointed out, the *Mystery* program concerns God's *secret purpose* for the heavens. Thus, when the appointed time arrived for its unveiling God raised up a new apostle to herald the good news. Of course, that man who was sent from God was Paul. God makes a very special case of his apostleship so that we might be able to clearly see the *difference* between the apostleship of the *twelve* and that of *Paul*.

The Lord draws our attention to the conversion of Paul in such a way that the child of God cannot help but grasp the paramount importance of the event. The better part of three chapters is devoted to the subject in the Book of Acts (Acts 9,22,26), followed by two more chapters in Galatians and I Timothy, which expand further on the truth of his coming to know Christ. No other conversion in all the Word of God is explained in such detail. The Holy Spirit rivets our attention to the salvation of Paul in order to teach us that there has been a change in the program of God. With Israel set aside in unbelief, the Twelve

Apostles were directed to announce to the little flock that the establishment of the kingdom was going to be temporarily withheld.

The Lord set His new program in motion by commissioning a *new* apostle to declare to the world that He was doing something new and different among the Gentiles. Subsequently, Paul was ordained to this divine office to preach Jesus Christ according to the revelation of the Mystery (Rom. 16:25; Eph. 3:1-3). This explains why he rightfully defended his apostleship from the attacks of false accusers.

WHO CHOSE PAUL?

"Paul, an apostle, (not of men, neither by man, but by Jesus Christ, and God the Father, who raised Him from the dead)" (Gal. 1:1).

This passage should settle once and for all the fact that Paul was *not* one of the *Twelve,* nor the *thirteenth* apostle of the kingdom. We are to understand instead that he received a *distinct ministry* from the glorified Lord of heaven to make known the riches of His grace among the Gentiles. This is precisely what the Spirit of God wants us to acknowledge as we read this passage.

Paul's apostleship is said to be *"not of men."* In other words, he was not ordained to his office through *human instrumentality.* In our day it is common for a young man, after preparing for the ministry, to be publicly ordained into the Lord's service. The elders who are summoned to such an honorable occasion declare by their presence that the candidate before them is called of God to preach the gospel.

The Apostleship and Message of St. Paul

In Paul's case, however, the Twelve did not assemble themselves together, nor did any other group for that matter, to elect him to his office. The Spirit goes on to reinforce this truth by stating, *"neither by man."* Here, undoubtedly, Paul refers to Peter, revealing to us that his apostleship was not initiated through *human channels.* Peter did *not say,* "Paul is well qualified to hold the position; I will give him my personal endorsement."

Unlike that of Matthias, Paul's apostleship is unique in that the Lord of glory *personally* appeared to him in a heavenly vision to call him to be a new apostle to dispense a new message, which had been kept secret since the world began (Acts 26:19; Col. 1:26).

PAUL AND MATTHIAS

"And they appointed two, Joseph called Barsabas, who was surnamed Justus, and Matthias" (Acts 1:23).

Of course, there are many in Christendom who would reject the conclusion we have drawn in the foregoing lines. We believe most of these are genuinely sincere believers who have followed the teachings of men without searching the Scriptures for themselves. The problem with blindly following the instruction of a man is that when he makes a wrong turn everyone following him goes down the same pathway of error. A good illustration of this would be those who teach that Peter was out of the will of God in appointing Matthias to the apostolic seat left vacant by Judas. They claim that Peter overstepped his bounds because God had intended Paul to be the twelfth apostle. We believe, however, that God is sovereign; consequently, man cannot undermine His purposes. "And all the inhabitants of the earth are reputed as nothing: and *He doeth according to His will* in the army of heaven, and among the inhabitants of the earth: and *none can stay His hand, or say unto Him, What doest Thou?"* (Dan. 4:35). If God had planned for Paul to be the twelfth apostle of the kingdom, *no one,* not even Peter, could have intervened. Furthermore, the *Holy Spirit's guidelines* that He sets forth here in Acts chapter one completely eliminate Paul from the picture.

Unlike the other believers in the upper room, Peter and the disciples had already received the Holy Spirit when our Lord appeared to them during His post-resurrection ministry (John 20:22). Being under the *complete* control of the Spirit meant that he was in the center of God's will in this important matter of business.

With Peter officiating, he imparts to those present in the upper room that it will be necessary for another disciple to fill the position vacated by the one who betrayed the Master. Two qualifications must be met by those to be considered for such a high calling. First of all, it had to be someone who had faithfully accompanied them during the *entire course* of the earthly ministry of Christ (Acts 1:21,22). The time frame is announced as *"beginning with John,"* because John the Baptist was the first to preach the kingdom at hand, which declared Christ to be the King of Israel (Luke 16:16; John 1:49). The period was to conclude with the nominee having faithfully followed Christ until His ascension to heaven—*"Unto that same day that He was taken up from us."* It was to be *until the ascension* because our Lord, by that point in time, had taught all the facets of the kingdom to come (Acts 1:3).

The second qualification that was binding on the candidate was that he must be an eyewitness of the resurrection of Christ in His *earthly ministry,* believing that He was *the* One to be seated on the throne of David. This meant that those being considered for this office must be capable of testifying that they had *seen* the resurrected Christ. Paul could not possibly have fulfilled either one of these two requirements. As we know, he was not even saved until years later (Acts 9).

PAUL IS NOT THE THIRTEENTH APOSTLE

"And they gave forth their lots; and the lot fell upon Matthias; and he was numbered with the eleven apostles" (Acts 1:26).

The search for candidates ended with only two being eligible to meet the stipulations set down by the Holy Spirit. With Barsabas and Matthias singled out, *they* cast lots endeavoring to discover the Lord's will as to which one *He* had chosen (vs. 24). This is another testimony to the sovereignty of God and human responsibility harmonizing like a symphony. *"The lot is cast into the lap; but the whole disposing thereof is of the Lord"* (Prov. 16:33). Unquestionably, the *human channel* was used by our Lord to appoint Matthias, because the plural pronoun *they* of vs. 23 refers directly to the 120 in the upper room.

"And he [Matthias] was numbered with the eleven." These words came not from the lips of Peter, but rather from Luke, who was led by the Spirit to record these events. From this point forward Matthias is always identified by the Spirit of God as being one of the Twelve (Acts 2:14; 6:2; I Cor. 15:7).

Some having accepted this truth conclude that Paul must then be the thirteenth apostle of the kingdom. This, however, would disrupt the numerical system of the prophesied program, thus breaking the continuity of the infallible Word of God. The number 12 is the number of governmental authority, which is permanently stamped on the house of Israel. There were 12 sons of Israel from which came the 12 tribes of Israel who were to have the Promised Land divided into 12 portions with 12 princes to rule over the tribes. Our Lord taught His disciples that they would sit on 12 thrones judging the 12 tribes of Israel (Matt. 19:28). For their faithfulness, they would also have the honor of their names being inscribed on the 12 foundations in the New Jerusalem (Rev. 21:14). Prophecy does NOT leave room for a thirteenth apostle!

If Paul is not the twelfth or even the thirteenth apostle of the kingdom, then where does his apostleship fit into the picture of Prophecy? It doesn't, nor did God ever intend it to! The glorified Lord of heaven appeared to Paul on the Damascus Road for the sole purpose of appointing him the *apostle to the Gentiles.* God stopped the prophetic clock just as the tribulation period approached, and ushered in a new program known as the *Mystery.* As we have previously stated, with this new program came a new apostle to proclaim it among the nations.

The number of the Mystery dispensation is ONE. There is *one* body, *one* Spirit, *one* hope of our calling, *one* Lord, *one* faith, *one* baptism, *one* Father and ONE APOSTLE— PAUL (Eph. 4:4-6). Paul's apostolic credentials to be the revelator of the grace of God are as follows: He had seen the resurrected Christ of heaven (I Cor. 9:1; Acts 26:16); the Corinthians were the fruits of his labor, being the seal of his apostleship (I Cor. 9:2); the signs of an apostle were evidenced in his ministry (II Cor. 12:12); Paul's instructions are said to be the commands of Christ for the Church, which is His body (I Cor. 14:37).

How we thank God for the Apostle Paul's ministry, through which we have come to understand the manifold wisdom of God! Until the Church at large comes to accept Paul's God-given authority it will continue to be tossed on the sea of confusion and be at the mercy of the traditions of men. Perhaps the following comparison of the apostleship of Paul and the Twelve will prove to be helpful:

The Twelve	*The One*
12 Apostles represented Israel	Paul is the Apostle to the Gentiles
Chosen by Christ on earth	Chosen by Christ from heaven
Preached the kingdom message which offered an earthly hope	Preached the gospel of the grace of God which offers a heavenly hope
Based on Prophecy & Covenants	Based on Grace
Scope—Palestine and the world through Israel	Scope—the World
The Great Commission	Commission of Reconciliation

PAUL'S UNIQUE MESSAGE

"But I certify you, brethren, that the gospel which was preached of me is not after man. For I neither received it of man, neither was I taught it, but by the revelation of Jesus Christ" (Gal. 1:11,12).

The Apostle Paul did not mince words when he wrote to the Galatians that the gospel he was preaching *"is not after man."* He sought to make it perfectly clear that his message was not conceived by him or anyone else. It can be properly said that most religions of the world have originated with some extremist who was deceived by Satan. The cruelties of Islam for example can be traced straight back to Mohammed, while the strange doctrines of Mormonism were largely propagated by Joseph Smith. Conversely, only Judaism and the gospel of the grace of God have been divinely ordained from above.

Insofar as Paul's gospel did not originate with man it logically follows that he neither received it nor was taught it through human channels. Therefore, we are to conclude that the apostle never majored in grace theology at the *University of Tarsus,* nor did he learn about the Mystery at the feet of Gamaliel while attending *Seminary* in Jerusalem.

Looking back on the corridor of divine revelation we know now that the dispensation of Grace was foreordained, but was a carefully guarded secret. Only God knew when and to whom He would make known the eternal counsels of His will for the heavens. Accordingly, one bright, sunny day on a dusty road leading to Damascus God chose to save a wretched sinner by the name of Saul. This divine intervention into the affairs of men marked the dawn of a *new era.* With one turn of the wheel, God set into motion a series of events that would change the course of history.

Paul's conversion experience is in itself an informative snapshot of the message he was being raised up to proclaim. For example, God waited to save Paul in sight of a *Gentile* city, which is representative of his forthcoming ministry among the *Gentiles* (Acts 26:16 cf. Rom. 11:13). Another significant feature is that our Lord appeared to the apostle-to-be in a *heavenly* vision. This, of course, launched the heavenly ministry of Christ, which offers the hope of *heaven* to all who believe (Acts 26:16-19 cf. Col. 1:5). Furthermore, Paul had seen the *Lord* in a blaze of glory as He had never been seen before. A short time later, he realized he had actually laid eyes on the *Lord of glory* who for the very *first* time revealed Himself as the Head of the Body of Christ (Acts 26:13-15 cf. Eph. 1:20-23; Col. 1:18). Also, prior to Paul's conversion he was breathing out threatenings and slaughter against all who named the name of Christ. He was God's foremost enemy. But rather than crush His enemy, God manifested His longsuffering and saved the leader of the rebellion who, incidentally, has become a pattern to all those who should hereafter believe on Christ (Acts 26:9-12 cf. I Tim. 1:15,16).

As we mentioned a moment ago, Paul did not receive his gospel through human means. Rather it was by *direct revelation* of the Lord Jesus Christ. It would have been impossible for Peter to teach Paul the Mystery, simply because he had absolutely no knowledge of it. This explains why the apostle is so adamant when he declares that he was called *"To reveal His [God's] Son in me, that I might preach Him among the heathen; immediately I conferred not with flesh and blood: neither went I up to Jerusalem to them which were apostles before me; but I went into Arabia, and returned again unto Damascus"* (Gal. 1:16,17).

In all probability the Lord appeared to Paul a number of times during his sojourn in Arabia where he received the A,B,C's of grace teaching. On another occasion he was caught up to the third heaven where the Lord personally tutored him further in the dimensions of the Mystery. These experiences indicate to us that he received the gospel of grace *progressively* over a period of about thirty years. This is what the apostle is speaking of in II Cor. 12:1 when he writes:

> "It is not expedient for me doubtless to glory. I will come to visions and revelations of the Lord."

WHY DID PAUL GO TO THE JEW FIRST?

In the early chapters of the Book of Acts God gave Israel a second chance to receive her Messiah. But one does not need to read very far to discover that she rejected God's gracious offer, desiring rather to persecute those who proclaimed the good news.

The leaders in Israel, embodied in the Sanhedrin, first *threatened* the apostles to discontinue their preaching that Jesus is the Christ who arose from the dead. When this failed, the council became more adamant, *beating* the disciples and threatening their very lives. However, the moment of truth came with the *murder* of Stephen. This brutal act spelled the setting aside of Israel as far as God was concerned. Therefore, the epitaph written over her house even to this day is *Lo-ammi* (not my people).

THE STONING OF STEPHEN

> "And Stephen, full of faith and power, did great wonders and miracles among the people. . . . And he said, Men, brethren, and fathers, hearken. . ." (Acts 6:8; 7:2).

The Apostleship and Message of St. Paul

Acts chapter seven unfolds Israel's great hour of crisis. The entire narrative centers around Stephen's final address to his countrymen and his subsequent death. For centuries God had been more than longsuffering with His chosen people, but now they had come to the hour of decision. We are told by Luke that Stephen was *"a man full of faith and of the Holy Spirit"* (Acts 6:5). And now his face shone *"as if it had been the face of an angel"* (6:15). Thus, to reject his message would be a serious matter indeed, for he was the channel through whom the Spirit was speaking. A casual reading of Acts seven reveals that Stephen carefully reviews the history of Israel. He very effectively points his hearers to two of their forefathers whom the entire nation had revered.

Like the master who strokes the canvas with his brush, Stephen presents the following argument to those present that fateful day: The first time that Joseph and Moses came to the brethren they were turned away. However, the second time that they came unto them they were received with thanksgiving. In essence, he is saying to his hearers: You have already rejected Christ once, why will you not *now* receive Him that the *Times of Refreshing* may be ushered in from the Father? Those whom Stephen was addressing were enraged that he would even think of relating Christ in any way to Joseph and Moses. Furthermore, they had already *falsely* made the accusation to the Sanhedrin that they heard him say *"... this Jesus of Nazareth shall destroy this place [that is, the temple at Jerusalem], and shall change the customs which Moses delivered us"* (Acts 6:13,14). Stephen, sensing their animosity, pronounced this indictment:

> "Ye stiffnecked and uncircumcised in heart and ears, ye do always resist the Holy Spirit: as your fathers did, so do ye" (Acts 7:51).

Interestingly, he goes on to add in verse 56:

> ". . . behold, I see the heavens opened, and the Son of Man standing on the right hand of God."

Talk about waving a red flag in front of a raging bull! These Jews were so infuriated upon hearing these words that they *"cast him out of the city"* and stoned him to death. Undoubtedly, they were familiar with the Psalm that states: *"Arise, O Lord, in Thine anger, lift up Thyself because of the rage of mine enemies; and awake for me to the judgment that Thou hast commanded"* (Ps. 7:6).

When Stephen saw the Son of Man *standing* at the right hand of God, it meant that the Lord was ready to pour out His wrath upon His enemies. But, these religious leaders were unwilling to acknowledge that they were the enemies of God. Therefore, they stoned God's servant to death, having convinced themselves that they were doing God a favor by ridding the nation of this blasphemer. Israel's response to God's Anointed One and to the offer of the kingdom was the stoning of Stephen. It was at this point in time that God set her aside in unbelief, for she was guilty of committing the *unpardonable sin* (Matt. 12:31,32). This helps to explain the Apostle Paul's words in Romans 11:11:

> "I say then, Have they [Israel, nationally] stumbled that they should fall [i.e. beyond recovery]? God forbid: but rather through their fall salvation is come unto the Gentiles, for to provoke them to jealousy."

> "For if the casting away of them be the reconciling of the world, what shall the receiving of them be, but life from the dead?" (Rom. 11:15).

We conclude then that God in His sovereignty pronounced Israel *excommunicated* at the stoning of Stephen. On the other hand, humanly speaking, the process of *casting away* the favored nation in a practical sense took approximately 30 years.

TO THE JEW FIRST

> "For I am not ashamed of the gospel of Christ: for it is the power of God unto salvation to every one that believeth; to the Jew first, and also to the Greek" (Rom. 1:16).

As we have seen, the gospel of Christ was presented to the Jew first, but they refused to believe. Therefore, God raised up the Apostle Paul and sent him to the Gentiles to preach Christ according to the revelation of the Mystery. We cannot overemphasize the fact that Paul received his commission to testify of the gospel of the grace of God the day he was saved on the road to Damascus (Acts 26:16,17 cf. Acts 20:24; Rom. 11:13). Incidentally, this can only mean that the apostle *never* proclaimed the kingdom gospel.

If Paul is the apostle to the Gentiles and is commissioned with a new message, then what possible explanation can we give for him going to the *Jew first* in his early ministry? The answer is twofold: First, it was a matter of *convenience*. The synagogue of the Jews was a natural place to begin, because there was always a gathering of those who feared God. One such example is found in Acts 13:15,16:

"And after the reading of the Law and the prophets the rulers of the synagogue sent unto them, saying, Ye men and brethren, if ye have any word of exhortation for the people, say on. Then Paul stood up, and beckoning with his hand said, men of Israel, and ye that fear God [GENTILES], give audience."

The apostle, of course, used such occasions to reach his countrymen for Christ, but it is interesting that it was the Gentiles who primarily heeded his words. As Paul closed his message on *Justification* at Antioch we are told that "... *when the Jews were gone out of the synagogue, the Gentiles besought that these words might be preached to them the next sabbath"* (Vs. 42).

The second and most significant reason that Paul went to the Jew first was to leave Israel *without excuse.* Bear in mind, God had removed His hand of blessing from Israel some years earlier. And who better to deliver the news that He has turned to the Gentiles than Paul? Thus, the apostle preaches the *good news* of Christ to his kinsmen after the flesh, hoping to reach some of them *individually* with the grace of God.

Moreover, he announced to them that they were being cast aside nationally in favor of a *Gentile* ministry. Needless to say, with most of them this went over like a *lead balloon!* In the minds of these religiously pious Jews, THEY were the people of God who had received the covenants, promises and the oracles of God!! Why, the audacity to insinuate otherwise was unthinkable. True, but when their Messiah *"came unto His own, His own received Him not"* (John 1:11). Hence, the following three pronouncements are delivered.

PAUL'S THREE PRONOUNCEMENTS

1. AT ANTIOCH

"Then Paul and Barnabas waxed bold, and said, It was necessary that the Word of God should first have been spoken to you: but seeing ye put it from you, and judge yourselves unworthy of everlasting life, lo, we turn to the Gentiles" (Acts 13:46).

The first *dictum of excommunication* upon Israel came at Antioch in Pisidia during Paul's first apostolic journey. This pronouncement was made in the *East* and we can be sure that word spread quickly to Jerusalem and the eastern regions beyond.

2. AT CORINTH

As the grace of God advanced westward the next declaration was made in *Europe* on Paul's second apostolic journey. Upon the apostle's arrival at Corinth he reasoned with the Jews that Jesus is the Christ. This does not run contrary to the gospel of the grace of God, but rather confirms it. We, too, have often spoken to our Hebrew friends to prove that Jesus is Israel's Messiah. Most Hebrews who are saved will tell you that the blessedness of their salvation has been realized in two ways: First, the Lord is their Savior and secondly, He is indeed Israel's Messiah.

The Jews at Corinth, though, would have none of this: *"And when they opposed themselves, and blasphemed, he shook his raiment, and said unto them. Your blood be upon your own heads; I am clean; from henceforth I will go unto the Gentiles"* (Acts 18:6).

3. AT ROME

As the circle broadens, at the end of Paul's third apostolic journey he was taken as a prisoner to Rome where he delivered his third and final pronouncement upon Israel. It was in the *West* that the apostle made one last attempt to plead with some of the prominent leaders of the Jewish community, but to no avail.

Paul says, *"For the heart of this people is waxed gross, and their ears are dull of hearing, and their eyes they have closed; lest they should see with their eyes, and hear with their ears, and understand with their heart, and should be converted. . . . Be it known therefore unto you, that the salvation of God is sent* [Gr. past tense] *unto the Gentiles, and that they will hear it"* (Acts 28:27,28). Little wonder that Judaism today is nothing but an empty shell. Some day soon God will turn again to Israel, but for now salvation is sent to the Gentiles. We should add that the farther *west* the gospel of grace has come the greater its impact. Compare, for example, the fruits of the gospel in America with the predominantly Muslim countries of the East, such as Iraq and Saudi Arabia. Of course, Christianity is the answer to all of the unrest in the Middle East.

There is nothing more gratifying to the heart than being in the center of God's will. Only here do we find true fulfillment. With this in mind, we shall forge ahead toward that yonder light which shines in the distance. That light is the preaching of *Jesus Christ* according to the revelation of the Mystery.

4
Dispensationalism

> "Whereof I am made a minister, according to the dispensation of God which is given to me for you, to fulfill the Word of God; Even the Mystery which hath been hid from ages and from generations, but now is made manifest to His saints."
> —*Colossians 1:25,26*

There has been quite an animated discussion of late on the subject of *dispensationalism*. John H. Gerstner, in his book *Wrongly Dividing the Word of Truth* goes to great lengths to discredit dispensationalism on the basis that it is a more recent phenomenon. In his thinking, since Covenant Theology, of which he is an able defender, can supposedly be traced back to the 2nd century it is obviously the most reliable method to interpret the Scriptures. We believe that such reasoning is flawed, to say the least.

One need only to read the writings of the Church Fathers to discover that they were all terribly confused. As we have seen, this should not surprise us when we remember that they had turned their backs on the apostleship and message of St. Paul (II Tim. 1:15).[1]

Insofar as Church history has sometimes proven itself to be an unreliable guide, one is wise to ask: What saith the Scriptures? Dr. Gerstner, in his haste to defend the traditional view of Covenant Theology, fails to see that the

---

1. Ibid. Page 9

Scriptures themselves set forth the system of interpretation called *dispensationalism*. Understanding the Word of God dispensationally is by far the most logical way to ascertain the eternal counsels of God. This allows the Scriptures to be interpreted *literally* unless the context clearly demands otherwise. Also, it alleviates the need to spiritualize certain passages in order to arrive at the proper sense.

DISTINGUISHING BETWEEN THE AGES AND DISPENSATIONS

"Now all these things happened unto them for ensamples: and they are written for our admonition, upon whom the ends of the world [AGES] are come" (I Cor. 10:11).

According to this passage, there are certain things recorded in the Old Testament which were meant to be a solemn warning to those living at the *close* of the Jewish age, as well as to those at the *beginning* of the present age. Here in one sweeping statement Paul singles out two ages. The term *age* (GR. AION) is to be understood as ". . . a period of indefinite duration or time viewed in relation to what takes place in the period." In other words, an age is a period of time with both a beginning and an ending, as the above passage plainly teaches.

When marking the divisions of the ages, dispensationalists tend to divide the pie somewhat differently depending on their theological persuasion. May we suggest the following:

1. The Age of Liberty (Gen. 1-3).

2. The Age of the Nations (Gen. 4-11).

3. The Age of the Jewish Nation (Gen. 12—Acts 8).

4. The Present Evil Age (Acts 9—Heb. 13 cf. Gal. 1:4).

5. The Kingdom Age (James 1—Rev. 20 cf. Matt. 24:3,14).

6. The Ages to Come (Eph. 2:7 cf. Rev. 21,22).

> "If ye have heard of the dispensation of the grace of God which is given me to you-ward: How that by REVELATION He made known unto me the Mystery. . ." (Eph. 3:2,3).

Within the framework of the ages God has manifested His will in what is commonly known as *dispensations*. A dispensation should never be regarded as a period of time, as its counterpart, although it is correct to say that it does cover time. The word simply means, ". . . a mode of dealing, an arrangement or administration of affairs." The only hope that mankind ever had of knowing the will of God was through direct revelations. These revelations were given or *dispensed* to holy men of God who were led by the Spirit. Although the attributes of God are *immutable* (unchangeable), sometimes God does *change* His dealings with man as we shall see in a moment.

Unfortunately, there is also disagreement among dispensationalists as to how many cuts should be made in the dispensational pie. Some believe that there are only *three* administrations, which are to be divided accordingly: Father, Son and Holy Spirit. This is an interesting concept, but it lacks Scriptural support. Moving to the other end of the spectrum, there are those who teach that there are as many as *twelve* dispensations. One is hard pressed, however, to defend this position. *Seven* dispensations is perhaps the most widely accepted view held by most Bible teachers. While we have no major objections to this view, it does seem to confuse time, as we know it, with the eternal state. Therefore, to help clarify the distinction, we hold the position that there are *eight* dispensations:

1. Dispensation of Innocence (Gen. 1:27,28).
2. Dispensation of Conscience (Gen. 3:7 cf. Rom. 2:14,15).
3. Dispensation of Human Government (Gen. 9:1-7).
4. Dispensation of Promise (Gen. 12:1-3; 13:14-17).
5. Dispensation of the Law (Ex. 19,20).
6. Dispensation of Grace (Eph. 3:1-6).
7. Dispensation of Divine Government (Ps. 2:1-12; Rev. 11:15-19; Rev. 20).
8. Dispensation of the Fulness of Times (Eph. 1:10).

It is interesting that each dispensation begins with a *probationary* period which serves as a time of testing. Thus, the course of each dispensation follows basically the same pattern: The dispensing of God's will; man's responsibility; man's failure; and God's judgment.

CORRELATING THE AGES AND THE DISPENSATIONS

The purpose of this chapter is to impart to the reader an outline of the dispensations, with special attention being given to where the present *dispensation of grace* fits into the overall picture. Perhaps the following will help give us some direction in this area:[2]

---

2. See graph on page 71.

Dispensationalism

I. **Age of Liberty** *(Dispensation of Innocence)*

   A. God was dealing with man in his innocence.

   1. Man created in the image of God (Gen. 1:26, 27).

   2. Man created to rule (Gen. 1:26,27).

   3. Man to be fruitful and multiply (Gen. 1:28).

   4. Perfect environment—Man was to be a vegetarian (Gen. 2:5,8,9).

   B. Man's responsibility was to guard the garden and to *abstain* from partaking of the tree of the knowledge of good and evil (Gen. 2:16,17).

   C. Man's failure came when Adam and Eve ate of the forbidden fruit, resulting in the entrance of sin and death (Gen. 3:6).

   D. Judgment—The pronouncement of the *curse* and expulsion from the garden (Gen.3:14-19,23,24).

It is noteworthy that even though God is no longer dealing with man in innocence, there are aspects of the original revelation given to Adam that are *still* binding today. For example, the command to be fruitful and multiply has never been rescinded and the consequence of sin remains the same—DEATH!

II. **The Age of the Nations** *(Dispensation of Conscience)*

   A. God dispensed conscience, which indicates that man had come to a knowledge of good and evil.

   1. Adam and Eve *knew* they were naked after they disobeyed God (Gen. 3:7).

2. The First Civilization (Gen. 4:16-24).

B. Now that conscience was to govern man, God required them to do good and refrain from all forms of evil (Gen. 3:22).

    1. God commanded Cain and Abel to bring a blood sacrifice to be accepted by Him (Gen. 4:1-4).

    2. God required *faith* (Heb. 11:4).

C. Cain disobeyed and in a jealous rage murdered his brother Abel (Gen. 4:5-15).

    1. Polygamy (Gen. 4:19).

    2. Violence filled the earth because men refused to heed their conscience (Gen. 6:13).

D. Judgment—The universal flood in the days of Noah (Gen. 6:17).

The believer today, of course, is not required to offer blood sacrifices or to build an ark. Everyone, however, does have a conscience and *knows* inwardly the basic difference between right and wrong (Rom. 2:14,15).

II. **Cont'd.** *(Dispensation of Human Government)*

A. God revealed that man was now to *govern,* which strongly implies the rise of nations.

    1. The fear of man is placed on the beast of the field (Gen. 9:2).

    2. Man is permitted to eat meat (Gen. 9:3).

    3. Human Government is established (Gen. 9:5,6).

B. Man bears the responsibility to establish laws that are in accordance with the righteous standard of God.

1. God's law states "Whosoever sheddeth man's blood, by man shall his blood be shed: for in the image of God made He man" (Gen. 9:6). Hence, the need for capital punishment.

2. "Be fruitful and multiply" should have resulted in the human race dispersing to the ends of the earth (Gen. 9:7).

C. If there is one thing the human race does consistently, it is to *fail*. And fail they did, when they sought to unite together and defy God's command to populate the earth (Gen. 11:4).

1. Their desire to BE KNOWN meant that they had neglected to implement a form of human government, which produced the spirit of lawlessness spoken of in Romans Chapter 1.

2. The erection of the so-called Tower of Babel was also in defiance of the Holy One of heaven as evil men desired to pay homage to the *astrological signs* of the heavens (Gen. 11:3,4 cf. Rom. 1:22,23).

D. God's judgment was swift as He confounded their language, thus forcing them to scatter abroad (Gen. 11:7-9).

III. **Age of the Jewish Nation** *(Dispensation of Promise)*

A. God dispensed a promise to Abraham that his seed would be multiplied as the stars of heaven.

1. The promise included:

    a. A *land* called Canaan that bordered the Nile River to the South and extended to the River Euphrates to the East (Gen. 15:17,18).

    b. A *nation* known as Israel (Gen. 12:2).

    c. Worldwide *blessing* (Gen. 12:3).

2. Circumcision was mandatory as a seal of the Abrahamic Covenant (Gen. 17:9-14).

B. The promise that God made with Abraham was *unconditional*.

1. Abraham's descendants were responsible to *trust* God to fulfill the promise (Gen. 26:1-4; 28:10-15).

2. With privilege always comes responsibility.

C. One lapse of faith after another seemed to plague the descendants of Israel in the early going.

1. Isaac for example, reluctantly obeyed the Word of the Lord not to go down to Egypt when a famine came upon the land. He did, however, move to Gerar, which is about as close to Egypt as one could get without actually being there (Gen. 26:1-6).

2. Jacob stole the birthright from Esau (Gen. 25:24-34).

3. Israel forsook the land of his forefathers and moved to Egypt (Gen. 41:54-57 cf. 46:26). This is a good example of the *permissive* will of God.

Dispensationalism

D. Judgment: God's chastisement was allowing Israel to remain in bondage to the Egyptians for 400 years. This made Israel appreciate more fully the forsaken Promised Land (Ex. 1:7-22).

III. **Cont'd.** *(Dispensation of the Law)*

A. God dispensed the Law to Moses.

1. The characteristics of the Law:

   a. Moral—The 10 Commandments were given to govern Israel's moral life (Ex. 20).

   b. Civil—This touched their social life, that is, how they were to act toward one another (Ex. 21).

   c. Ceremonial—Provided a means whereby they could make atonement for their sins. Here their religious life was in view (Lev. 16).

2. The purpose of the Law was to give Israel a knowledge of sin (Rom. 3:20).

B. Since the Covenant of the Law was *conditional,* those who were placed under it were responsible to keep *all* 613 commandments.

1. The blessing of God could be realized only IF they obeyed the voice of the Lord (Ex. 19:3-7).

2. Israel's willingness to accept the challenge soon proved to be a yoke about her neck (Ex. 19:8 cf. Acts 15:10).

C. Israel's failures under the Law are almost too numerous to consider.

1. Idol Worship (Ex. 32:1-6).
2. Unbelief (Num. 13:26-33).
3. Murmuring (Num. 16:1-8).
4. Fornication (Num. 25:1-3).
5. The words of Jeremiah sum it up well (Jer. 31:32).

D. Judgment: Historically, Israel experienced a number of serious judgments of God over the 1500 year period she was under the Law. Perhaps the most devastating calamities that befell her were:

1. The Assyrian Captivity (II Kings 17:4-6, 15-18).
2. The Babylonian Captivity (II Chron. 36:11-21).
3. The setting aside of the nation in unbelief at the stoning of Stephen (Acts 7).

IV. **The Present Evil Age** *(Dispensation of Grace)*

A. God dispenses *grace* to a lost and dying world (Eph. 3:2).

1. A new creation is brought into existence, known as the Church, the Body of Christ, which is made up of Jews and Gentiles without distinction (II Cor. 5:17; Eph. 1:22,23; 2:14-17).
2. Christ is the Head of the Body and holds a position of exaltation as He carries out His heavenly ministry (Eph. 1:20-23; Phil. 2:9; Col. 1:18).

Dispensationalism

3. Believers are baptized spiritually into one Body by the Spirit (I Cor. 12:13; Eph. 4:5).

4. We are no longer under the Law, but under GRACE. The abolition of the Law means that there are *no* ordinances to be observed during this administration (Rom. 6:14; Col. 2:14-17).

5. The Rapture of the Church is imminent (I Thes. 1:10; 4:13-18; Titus 2:13).

B. Members of Christ's Body are responsible to preach Jesus Christ according to the revelation of the Mystery (Rom. 16:25; I Cor. 9:16-18).

1. Believers today are to do the work of an evangelist (II Tim. 4:5).

2. Believers are called with a holy calling, and are to walk according to the Spirit, not according to the flesh (Rom. 12:1,2; Gal. 5:16-26).

C. The Church today has failed miserably to even acknowledge the Mystery, let alone making it known.

1. May God help us not to repeat the same mistake as the early members of the Body of Christ when they forsook Paul's message (II Tim. 1:15).

2. Thankfully, time still remains "to make all men see what is the fellowship of the Mystery" (Eph. 3:9).

D. Judgment: At the sounding of the trump, the members of Christ's Body will *all* appear before the Judgment Seat of Christ. A thorough review will be made of our lives to determine whether or not we have been faithful to the message of Grace that God called us to proclaim (Rom. 14:10; I Cor. 3:9-17; II Cor. 5:10,11).

This present dispensation should be of special interest to each of our readers since the preceding instructions are *our marching orders.* We trust that the Body of Christ will not follow in the footsteps of unbelief as did those of former dispensations. May we learn from their failures and heed the warnings that are committed to us by our apostle, lest we fall prey to the same (I Cor. 10:1-15).

V. **The Kingdom Age** *(Dispensation of Divine Government)*

   A. God *dispenses wrath* and *justice* on a Christ-rejecting world (Ps. 2:1-12).

      1. The Prophetic program will resume. Once again the Jewish nation will be in view (Rev. 7:1-8).

      2. The *tribulation* is a prelude to the coming millennial kingdom. The chief goal is to overthrow the kingdoms of this world and establish the kingdom of His dear Son (Rev. 11:15). This shall be accomplished by chastening Israel, punishing the nations, and bringing the time of Jacob's trouble to a close with the Second Coming of Christ (Jer. 30:7; Isa. 24:1; Ezek. 38:14-23; Matt. 24:29,30).

      3. The kingdom reign of the Messiah—Duration is 1000 years (Rev. 20:4,5,7).

Dispensationalism

      a. Throne of David is to be established (II Sam. 7:16; Matt. 19:28; Acts 2:30).

      b. Justice will fill the earth (Jer. 23:5,6).

      c. Peace will prevail (Isa. 9:6,7).

      d. Abrahamic and Davidic Covenants will be fulfilled.

B. Israel will be required to declare that Christ is indeed the *Messiah* of Israel.

    1. Certain aspects of the Law must again be observed, such as the Sabbath (Matt. 24:20).

    2. Repentance and Baptism will again be preached (Mark 16:15,16; Acts 2:38 cf. Rev. 9:21).

C. In the face of almost unbelievable judgment, men will choose rather to blaspheme God, who has the power to deliver them (Rev. 16:11,21).

    1. Man's failure will continue through the kingdom as sin from time to time will rear its ugly head (Isa. 65:20).

    2. Marvel of all marvels, after our Lord Jesus Christ rules in righteousness for a period of 1000 years there will be those who shall rise up in rebellion at the close of the millennium and challenge His authority (Rev. 20:7-9).

D. Judgment: Inasmuch as the kingdom is the consummation of the age, and time as we know it, there are a number of judgments:

1. Preceding the millennial kingdom, Israel will be judged (Matt. 25:14-30).
2. The nations shall be judged at this time as well (Matt. 25:31-46).
3. The Great White Throne—All the unsaved of all ages are summoned to the Throne of God where they are condemned to the eternal flame (Rev. 20:11-15).

E. The *Day of the Lord* closes with the heavens and earth consumed in fire as God prepares to execute his eternal purpose (II Peter 3:10).

VI. **The Ages to Come** *(Dispensation of the Fulness of Times)*

A. God's ultimate purpose for His creation is to sum up all things in Christ (Eph. 1:10).

1. The renovation of the heavens and the earth will return them to their pristine beauty (Ps. 104:5; Isa. 65:17; II Peter 3:11,12; Rev. 21:1).
2. The Body of Christ will reign with Christ throughout all eternity in the heavenlies (Eph. 2:6,7).
3. Israel and the redeemed of the Prophetic program will reign with Christ from the New Jerusalem on the new earth (Rev. 21:9-27).

B. All saints will live in harmony with one another and in all probability heaven and earth will be open to each other, since all things have been summed up in Christ.

1. Even in eternity we will serve the Lord with gladness (II Cor. 5:9).
2. God will be all in all (I Cor. 15:27,28).

C. NO MORE FAILURE, SIN, DEATH, TEARS OR PAIN—Hallelujah!!

D. NO MORE JUDGMENT: "And God shall wipe away all tears...and there shall be no more death ...for the former things are passed away" (Rev. 21:4).

FURTHER CLARIFICATION ON THE ETERNAL STATE

"That in the dispensation of the fulness of times He might gather together in one all things in Christ, both which are in heaven, and which are on earth; even in Him" (Eph. 1:10).

There are essentially two positions concerning *when* the *dispensation of the fulness of times* will actually take place. Some have laid claim to the idea that the phrase refers to the *Rapture,* while others say it points to a future day beyond this glorious event, as the foregoing outline advocates. It never ceases to amaze me how two believers can study the exact same passage and come up with completely different conclusions. This is why it is important to be Bereans, lest we find ourselves caught between two conflicting opinions.

It is well worth remembering that while a Pastor's obligation is to teach the Word, it is the responsibility of all believers to "search the Scriptures daily, whether those things be so." At the Judgment Seat of Christ, please don't say, "But Pastor Sadler said...!" If you come to the same conclusion I have on the *Dispensation of the Fulness of Times,* it should be because you are convinced in your own mind that this indeed is what the Scriptures teach.

APPOINTMENT WITH DESTINY

> "In Whom also we have obtained an inheritance, being predestinated according to the purpose of Him who worketh all things after the counsel of His own will" (Eph. 1:11).

It is our conviction that the phrase *Dispensation of the Fulness of Times* is a direct reference to the *eternal state*. According to the above passage God has *predestinated* the Body of Christ to partake in His eternal purpose for the heavens. Sadly, to many *predestination* is a harsh doctrine which should be avoided because of the controversy surrounding it. One very significant observation we need to make about this term is that *every time* it is used in the Scriptures it is always associated with the believer and *never* with the unbeliever.

Breaking the word *predestination* apart we are to understand that the prefix "pre" simply means beforehand. I am sure most are familiar with what is known as the "pre-game" show before a ball game. Before the game begins, the announcers usually evaluate the teams and interview key players. This is why it is called the "pre-game" show—it goes *before* the sporting event.

"Destination" basically means, where you are going to end up. For example, when I was a young man in high school I worked at the Carnegie Museum in Pittsburgh. Every day after school I would board a streetcar at Negley Ave. Since there were so many streetcars that traveled to town I had to be very careful to catch the correct one. I

Dispensationalism

was looking for the one which had the sign overhead "Oakland-Carnegie Museum" which was my *destination*.

Before the foundation of the world God had *predetermined* that the members of the Body of Christ would inherit the heavens. While the Rapture of the Church will be an essential part *toward* bringing the plans and purposes of God to completion, it cannot (in and of itself) be said to be the culmination of them. Surely the heavenly program of God could not be summed up in Christ at the Rapture in light of the Judgment Seat of Christ which is yet to follow. This event undoubtedly will cover a period of time which is only known to the Lord (II Cor. 5:10).

We must not forget that years after our home-going the heavens, as we know them, will still be occupied by the powers of darkness. Subsequently, in the middle of the tribulation period evil and rebellion will utterly consume both men and angels. At the appointed time Michael and his angels will march out of the heavenlies to make a declaration of war on these forces of evil. The ensuing battle will result in Satan's expulsion from the heavenly realms, which rightfully belong to us.

> "And there was war in heaven: Michael and his angels fought against the dragon; and the dragon fought and his angels, and prevailed not; neither was there place found any more in heaven. And the great dragon was cast out, that old serpent, called the devil, and Satan, which deceiveth the whole world: he was cast out into the earth, and his angels were cast out with him" (Rev. 12:7-9).

Furthermore, as the tribulation draws to a close the heavens will be the backdrop for a display of God's wrath such as this world has never known. These events were foretold by the prophets of old and reiterated by Peter on the day of Pentecost.

"And I will show wonders in heaven above, and signs in the earth beneath; blood, and fire, and vapor of smoke: the sun shall be turned into darkness, and the moon into blood, before that great and notable day of the Lord come" (Acts 2:19,20).

As we have seen, even though the curse will be *largely* lifted during the kingdom age to follow, the effects of sin will *still* be evident in God's universe.

DELIVERANCE

"Looking for and hasting unto the coming of the day of God, wherein the heavens being on fire shall be dissolved, and the elements shall melt with fervent heat? Nevertheless we, according to His promise, look for new heavens and a new earth, wherein dwelleth righteousness" (II Peter 3:12,13).

The *Day of God* will usher in the *Dispensation of the Fulness of Times* bringing us to the eternal state. As we know the day of Divine Retribution will close with the heavens and earth being consumed with fire, thus preparing them for the completion of God's plans and purposes. With eternity in view *all* the children of God will have been removed from the presence of sin and brought into a glorified state. Death, which is our last enemy, will be abolished and cast into the Lake of Fire along with those who have defiled themselves in unbelief.

At this point, God is going to renovate the old order, restoring it to its original beauty. This claims a moment of close attention for us to understand that God *"laid the foundations of the earth, that it should not be removed forever"* (Ps. 104:5). When Peter speaks about new heavens and a new earth he uses the Greek word *"Kainos"* (new) which indicates, not new in time, but new as to form or quality. Having accomplished this God will sum up all things in Christ, both which are in heaven and on the earth.

For the Body of Christ this means taking full possession of the new heavens, which is our part in the inheritance. Like the Apostle Paul we will be seated with Christ in all His glory so that throughout eternity the heavenly host may observe the trophies of God's grace. But there is more, much more; the Lord is also going to show His kindness to *us* in the ages to come (Eph. 1:3,11; 2:6,7; 3:10,11). To think that we are a glorious part of all of this in Christ! It should cause us to bow our knees in humble adoration.

The prophetic saints, of course, will inherit the earth which also will be delivered from the bondage of corruption. Apparently the New Jerusalem will become the capital of the new earth. Those who enter through the twelve gates of the city will behold the names of the *twelve tribes* of Israel written above. The crystal city will also have twelve foundations with the names of the *twelve Apostles* inscribed thereon as stated in the last chapter. This superstructure will be a stunning fifteen hundred mile cube and shall not require the light of the sun, for the Lord God Himself will be the sustaining light (Rev. 21:9-21; 22:1-5). Abraham's search for a city "whose builder and maker is God" will find fulfillment in the New Jerusalem.

A CLOSING THOUGHT

Throughout the ages and dispensations God has placed man under different circumstances to demonstrate that even in the most ideal conditions, such as the kingdom, man is basically at enmity with God and is in need of a Savior. Therefore, God's ultimate purpose in having us view His Word through the lens of dispensationalism is that we might see more clearly His *triumph over sin in the universe.*

With the dawn of eternity *all* will enjoy the glory of God's presence as we worship Him in true holiness. At long last peace, righteousness and holiness will prevail throughout the ages to the praise of His glory.

THE AGES AND DISPENSATIONS

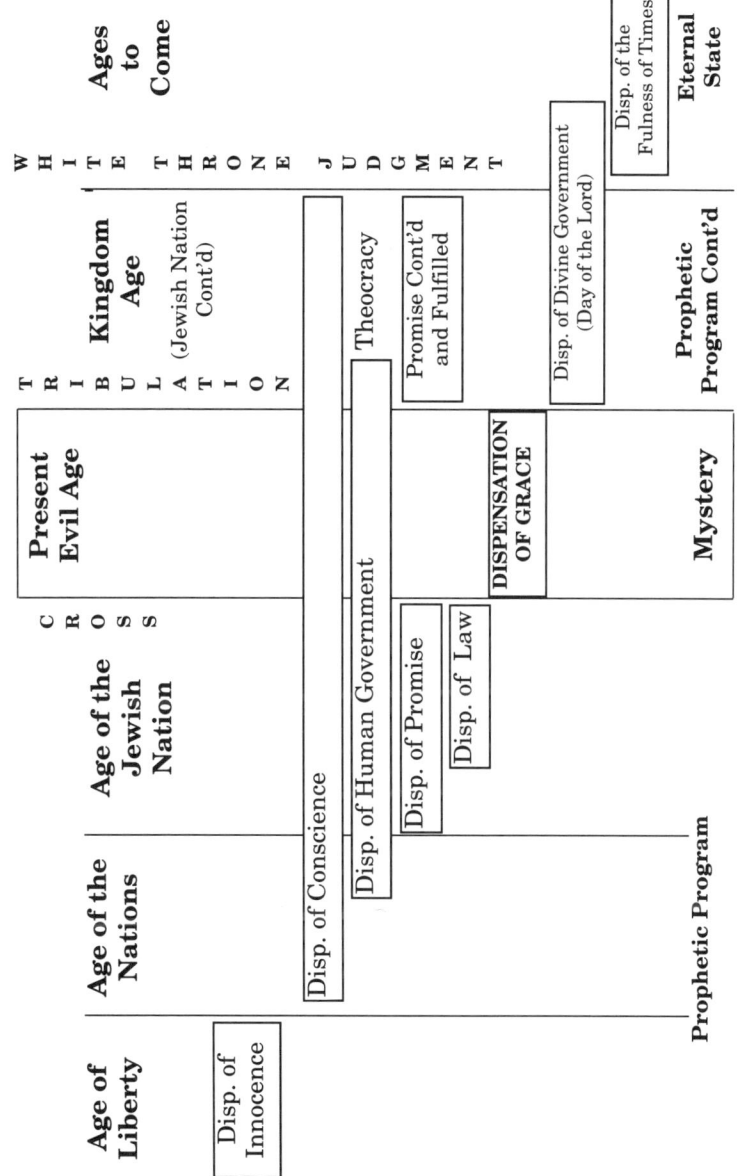

5
Characteristics of the Mystery

"For this cause I Paul, the prisoner of Jesus Christ for you Gentiles, if ye have heard of the dispensation of the grace of God which is given me to you-ward: How that by revelation He made known unto me the Mystery...."
—*Ephesians 3:1-3*

One of the most tried-and-true weapons in the war against crime is the common, everyday fingerprint. In 1901, Scotland Yard introduced the *Galton-Henry* system of fingerprint classification, which is still widely used by law enforcement agencies today. The reason this method has been so successful in the apprehension of criminals is because no two individuals have identical fingerprints. Thus, the impression made by the ridges on the ends of your fingers is *unique* to you alone.

In like manner, there are certain characteristics about the *Mystery* that distinguish it from God's former program of Prophecy. For those who have joined us in our quest for the truth, it will be advantageous for us to explore these *unique traits,* especially in view of the injunction of Holy Scripture: "... *be ready always to give an answer to every man that asketh you a reason of the hope that is in you with meekness and fear."*

THE SECRET

What is the Mystery? The *Mystery* is a divine program

Characteristics of the Mystery

which unveils the doctrines of grace solely intended for the Church, the Body of Christ. This program, of course, was *purposely withheld* from the prophetic saints who had preceded the Apostle Paul. W. E. Vine defines the term "Mystery" from the original language in the following way: ". . . it denotes, not the mysterious (as with the English word), but that which, being outside the range of unassisted natural apprehension, can be made known only by divine revelation, and is made known in a manner and at a time appointed by God. . . ." Thayer adds it is "a hidden purpose, counsel or secret will of God."

This helps to explain why Paul calls his message the *unsearchable riches of Christ* (Eph. 3:8). In other words, the doctrines of grace that the apostle received by direct revelation are not found anywhere else outside of his epistles. One need not be a theologian to understand that Paul's message of grace is unsearchable or *untrackable* in the annals of the old economy.

The writer knows firsthand something about the significance of this word. Back in the early 70's while attending Bible School, my family and I were unexpectedly caught in a blizzard. Approximately one-half mile from home, the snow had accumulated so rapidly that our car would proceed no farther. It took a few moments to regain my composure from the fear of what could happen under such circumstances. After a brief discussion we decided that I should try to walk a little distance from the car to see if it was possible to make it the rest of the way home on foot. About 25 yards down that deserted back road it became evident this would be an impossibility. As I turned around to follow my tracks back to the car, I was surprised

73

to find that the blowing snow had completely covered my footprints so quickly. My steps to a safe haven were *untrackable!* Unable to see my hand in front of my face, I thank God to this day for His protective care in returning me safely to my family.

Let's take a few moments to consider some of the unsearchable riches of Christ, which are found in the writings of St. Paul alone:

A *new apostolic office* is decreed by God as a channel to make known the *secret* of His will. Paul, of course, was the one divinely chosen to this office and was declared by the Holy Spirit to be the Apostle to the Gentiles (Rom. 11:13; I Cor. 1:1; Eph. 3:1,7,8).

A *new creation* is introduced known as the Church, the Body of Christ. This living organism is made up of Jews and Gentiles who have been reconciled together in one Body by the Cross. In the dispensation of Grace then, God is saving souls out of every nation and is sovereignly placing them together into Christ (I Cor. 12:13; II Cor. 5:17; Eph. 2:11-16).

A *new role* is assumed by our Lord Jesus Christ as well. Today He is portrayed as the Head of the Body, giving it spiritual life and purpose to the praise of His glory. What Christ meant to Israel as their King, He means to us as our Head (Eph. 1:20-23; 5:23,24; Col. 1:18).

A *new baptism* also emerges from the inspired pen of the apostle. He describes it as our *one baptism* into Christ, which is performed by the operation of the Holy Spirit who spiritually identifies us with Christ's death, burial and resurrection. Furthermore, upon the moment

Characteristics of the Mystery

of belief, this sovereign act places us into the Body of Christ where we are sealed with the Holy Spirit until the day of redemption (I Cor. 12:12,13; Eph. 1:13-15; 4:5).

A *new set of terms* are set forth in salvation. Paul is the first to proclaim the *good news* of Calvary, how that Christ died for our sins and rose again. In Paul's gospel alone, sinners are saved by grace through faith apart from the works of repentance and the law (Rom. 4:5; I Cor. 15:3,4; Eph. 2:8,9).

A *new commission* of reconciliation is dispensed, thus temporarily interrupting the Great Commission assigned to Israel. Our God-given responsibility is to go forth and tell this lost and dying world that God was in Christ Jesus reconciling the world unto Himself. Presently, in the age of Grace, God is no longer imputing their sins unto them and therefore they can be wonderfully saved simply by receiving His gracious offer of reconciliation (II Cor. 5:14-20; Col. 1:21-23; Rom. 5:6-11).

A *new expectation* is also imparted to the Church, which is His body. It is called the "Blessed Hope." Only the Apostle Paul addresses the Secret Coming of Christ for the members of His Body. Consequently, our hope is both heavenly in sphere and position (I Thes. 4:13-18; Titus 2:13; Eph. 2:4-7).

These few morsels are but a small sampling of the distinctive characteristics of the Pauline revelation. Like my footsteps that could not be found in the snow, Paul's *grace teachings* are UNTRACKABLE in the pages of Prophecy! Does this mean that we should shun the rest of the Bible? God forbid! We should, however, study all Scriptures in light of those things that were committed to the Apostle of the Gentiles.

A CONTROVERSIAL PASSAGE

Those of the Acts 2 camp argue that the Mystery was made known to ages and generations past, but not as fully as it is now revealed to his apostles and prophets. In other words, Paul was not the first to receive it. They base this conclusion on Ephesians 3:5, *"Which in other ages was not made known unto the sons of men as it now revealed unto His holy apostles and prophets by the Spirit."*

The proper exegesis of this passage hinges on the phrase *"as it is now revealed."* Therefore, we must determine whether the term "as" is used in the *comparative* or the *contrastive* sense. Perhaps an illustration will prove to be helpful: I might say: My golf game is *as* good *as* yours. Here the "as" is used in the comparative sense—I am comparing your game with mine. Turning to the contrastive side of our term we might say: The ancient Egyptians did not have computers *as* we do today. Applying our illustration to the passage in question we have two possibilities:

1) The Mystery was revealed prior to Paul, but not *as* (comparative) fully as it is today.

2) The Mystery was not revealed to ages and generations past *as* (contrastive) it is today through Paul's gospel.

The Acts 2 dispensationalists opt for number one. Those of us who have come to see Paul's distinctive ministry defend number two; thus, we have two opinions—but who is to say which one is correct? We are reminded at such times of the thought-provoking words of Elijah: "How long halt ye between two opinions?" The solution lies in the answer to the question, "What saith the Lord?" The following passages prove beyond a shadow of a doubt that the "as" is used in the *contrastive* sense in Ephesians 3:5, which can only mean the revelation of the Mystery was initially committed to Paul.

> "Now to Him that is of power to establish you according to my [Paul's] gospel, and the preaching of Jesus Christ according to the revelation of the Mystery, which has been KEPT SECRET since the world began" (Rom. 16:25).
>
> "If you have heard of the dispensation of the grace of God which is given me [Paul] to you-ward: how that by revelation He made known unto me the Mystery. . . . And to make all men see what is the fellowship of the Mystery, which from the beginning of the world hath been HID in God, who created all things by Jesus Christ" (Eph. 3:2,9).

So then, while Paul received the Mystery by direct *revelation* from the Lord of glory, the apostles and prophets, and those since, have received it through the *illumination* of the Spirit (Gal. 1:11,12 cf. Eph. 3:5). A knowledge of this glorious message is only obtainable through the enlightenment of the Holy Spirit. And it has been our experience that those who are in search of the key that unlocks the sacred secret are never denied access.

OTHER MYSTERIES

> "He answered and said unto them [His Hebrew disciples], Because it is given unto you to know the

mysteries of the kingdom of heaven, but to them [unbelieving Israel] it is not given" (Matt. 13:11).

It is often brought to our attention that there are countless references to the Mystery throughout the New Testament. We are unsure that "countless" is the correct term in view of the fact that the word *mystery* (Gr. *Musterion*) is only mentioned 27 times in the so-called New Testament—20 of which are found in Paul's writings. When the term *mystery* is used in the Prophetic Scriptures it is, *without exception,* relative to the earthly millennial kingdom. For example, the "mystery" of the wheat and tares in Matthew 13:24-30 is to be interpreted accordingly:

The sower is the Son of Man (Messiah). The field is the world where the *kingdom gospel* will one day reach every campfire. The good seed that was sown is believing Israelites who have placed their faith in the King. The tares are a reference to unbelieving Israel (Scribes, Pharisees, Sadducees, Essenes, etc.), who have rejected the counsel of God against themselves. The enemy is Satan and the harvest is the end of the world; that is, the end of this world system when the Son of Man will return in His Second Coming to engage the Anti-Christ in the battle of Armageddon. *"Then shall the righteous [prophetic saints] shine forth as the sun in the kingdom [millennial] of their Father. Who hath ears to hear, let him hear"* (Matt. 10:5-7; 13:36-43; 24:4-31; Luke 7:29,30).

Consequently, references to a "mystery" in the Prophetic program are *always* relative to the kingdom, whereas when Paul uses the term he is speaking of God's secret purpose, or some aspect thereof, for the Body of Christ.

THE MYSTERY AND THE VOLUME OF THE BOOK

"Whereof I am made a minister, according to the dispensation of God which is given to me for you, to fulfill the Word of God" (Col. 1:25).

The apostle makes a profound statement here when he says that it was given to him to fulfill or *complete* the Word of God. Even though this is a well established fact, we can hear a voice shouting from the gallery: Didn't the Apostle John complete the volume of the Book when he penned the Apocalypse? Indeed he did, in one sense of the word. Perhaps an illustration here will be helpful:

I'm sure we can all remember back when we were young and everyone had their own daily chores. It was window duty for yours truly when I visited my great-grandmother. She loved clean windows! I can still see her standing in the kitchen doorway drying her hands on her apron as she uttered, "How do these windows get so dirty?" I often wondered the same thing! But I also knew that this was the signal to find a pail and get busy. Like most kids that age, I enjoyed playing in the water and, for the most part, had it down to a science. It was great fun to fill a bucket near the top and see if you could reach the rag in the bottom of the bucket without making it overflow! The trained eye, when choosing the proper water level had to account for the water rising in the pail while at the same time being forced to the sides. One miscalculation and you had a real mess to clean up in grandma's kitchen. Water, then, fills a bucket from bottom to top (depth) and from side to side (breadth)

In similar fashion, the same is true of the Word of God. When the Apostle John *completed* his writings he put the finishing touches on the Prophetic Scriptures by giving them *depth*. In the Book of Revelation, John simply added more detail to what had already been foretold in prophecy. He also placed the events of the end time in a chronological order, something which had not been done prior to his writing.

On the other hand, in the parenthetical period between the setting aside of the nation Israel and the coming events of the tribulation, God announced a new program to show forth the riches of His grace. Of course, at God's *appointed time* He made known to the Apostle Paul the secret counsel of His will, which is now recorded for us in his epistles. Therefore, Paul completed the Word of God in its *breadth* and he tells us that he accomplished this by filling it with the *Mystery*

> ". . . which is given to me [Paul] for you, to fulfill the Word of God; even the Mystery which had been hid from ages and from generations, but now is made manifest to His saints" (Col 1:25,26)

The next time you fill that pail with water may it bring to mind the wonderful Word of God that enriches our lives. Little wonder that while meditating on his new revelation, the apostle broke forth with this touching doxology in the Book of Romans: *"O the depth of the riches both of the wisdom and knowledge of God! How unsearchable are His judgments and His ways past finding out!"* Before the foundation of the world God had foreordained that the Gentiles should be fellow heirs with Christ, and marvel of marvels, He kept it a secret for 4,000 years, but thanks be unto God it is *now* made manifest.

A SUPPLEMENTARY WORD

So that the reader will not become confused when studying Paul's epistles, the apostle frequently uses various titles when referring to the special revelation he received from the Lord of glory. These titles are often used interchangeably, but it is important to acknowledge that each one describes some important aspect of his divine message.

1. The Mystery—Eph. 3:3
2. The revelation of the Mystery—Rom. 16:25
3. The gospel of the grace of God—Acts 20:24
4. The gospel of the uncircumcision—Gal. 2:7
5. My gospel—II Tim. 2:8
6. The faith—II Tim. 4:7
7. The glorious gospel or the gospel of the glory— I Tim. 1:11
8. The unsearchable riches of Christ—Eph. 3:8

The *Mystery,* like the fingerprint, is stamped with unique features that distinguishes it from all the other plans and purposes of God. Unfortunately, *tradition* has obscured the spiritual sight of many believers from seeing the simplicity of Paul's gospel. May God help us increasingly to be Bereans and study to see if these things be so!

> "Love's redeeming work is done.
> Fought the fight, the battle won
> Death in vain forbids Him rise
> Christ has opened paradise."
> —Charles Wesley

6
The Two Ministries of Christ

> "Now I say that Jesus Christ was [not is] a minister of the circumcision for the truth of God, to confirm the promises made unto the fathers."
> —Romans 15:8

As we arrive at this stage in our analysis of the *Unsearchable Riches of Christ* we trust that our readers are at least beginning to see the importance of rightly dividing the Word of truth. This is the key to understanding and enjoying the Scriptures. Those who show an intolerance toward properly dividing the Word of God are going to be inconsistent in their conclusions.

Sadly, they must resort to questionable tactics, such as spiritualizing the Scriptures in order to explain difficult passages. For example, before our Lord's ascension He emphatically told His disciples to *begin* at Jerusalem in their proclamation of the kingdom gospel. Moreover, they were to proceed no further until the upper echelon of Israel's leadership was converted to Messiah. We are told by some, however, that Jerusalem isn't really Jerusalem, but Chicago or wherever one may live. If you reside in Chicago then this is your Jerusalem. I don't know where you live, but Chicago is geographically a long distance from Jerusalem. Even more importantly, the reason our Lord commanded His disciples to begin at Jerusalem has absolutely nothing to do with the city of Chicago. Nor does this have anything whatsoever to do with the gospel of the grace of God.

Beloved, if we rightly divide the Word of truth according to II Timothy 2:15 we are in a position to leave the Scriptures in their natural setting. Thus, it is never necessary to twist passages to make them say something God never intended them to say. With this in mind, before we engage in a discussion on the sevenfold unity of the Spirit, perhaps it would be advantageous for us to consider the *two* ministries of Christ.

CHRIST'S EARTHLY MINISTRY

Paul affirms that when our Lord entered the human arena He purposely limited His ministry to those of the circumcision. Read Rom. 15:8 again. In short, His visitation was explicitly to Israel in order to substantiate the promises that were given to Abraham, Isaac and Jacob. Since the Hebrew fathers rejoiced in an earthly hope, it goes without saying that our Lord's earthly ministry is woven throughout the pages of prophecy. Due to Israel's obstinacy, this ministry is presently *inoperative.* Today, our Lord is carrying out His *heavenly ministry* which relates to the Body of Christ. Sad to say, many are *trying* their level best to walk in the footsteps of Christ's earthly ministry. Of course, they can do no more than try because it is impossible to follow directions that were never meant for us in the first place.

> "Then spake Jesus to the multitude, and to His disciples, Saying, The scribes and the Pharisees sit in Moses' seat: All therefore whatsoever they bid you observe, that observe and do; but do not ye after their works: for they say, and do not" (Matt. 23:1-3).

As our Lord's earthly ministry to Israel was drawing to

a close, He imparted the so-called Great Commission.[1] In this commission He taught them to "... *observe all things whatsoever I have commanded you: and, lo, I am with you always, even unto the end of the world"* (Matt. 28:20). One of the essentials of the faith the Master had delivered unto them was the necessity of *obeying* those who sit in Moses' seat. If we carefully examine a slice of the four gospels we learn that Christ and His followers meticulously kept the feast days as required in the Book of Leviticus. When the Great Physician healed the poverty stricken leper from his leprosy, He demanded that he present himself, with a sacrifice, to the priest who alone had the *authority* to pronounce him clean (Matt. 8:1-4). This compelling evidence establishes that our Lord lived under the Law and further explains why His disciples were commanded to strictly adhere to the Law of Moses.

Thankfully, with the setting aside of Israel in unbelief we are no longer under the Law, but under *grace*. Perhaps a segment of our readers who do not know the Mystery are thinking: Well, I believe that! Good! Then who brought us this wonderful truth? It was none other than Paul himself, who received this *new* revelation from the Lord of glory (Rom. 6:14,15).

Those who are struggling to live in accordance with the earthly ministry of Christ, which includes the early Acts record, are inadvertently placing themselves back under the Law. As we have seen, believers today cannot possibly follow the commands of Christ to Israel, simply because

---

1. Every commission of God falls under the classification of "great," although the greatest commission of all is that of *reconciliation* given to Paul.

the nation has been temporarily set aside. All that remains is an empty shell of what once was (Rom. 11:31, 32). There are no religious leaders sitting in Moses' seat to obey. The temple is nonexistent and the priesthood a relic of the past. It is indeed perplexing that so many believers are like sheep, following one another through the ruins of God's abandoned program of Prophecy. Our heart's desire is that all believers everywhere will come to a knowledge of the Mystery!

THE HEAVENLY MINISTRY OF CHRIST

> "But rise, and stand upon thy feet: for I have appeared unto thee for this purpose, to make thee a minister and a witness both of these things which thou hast seen, and of those things in the which I will appear unto thee" (Acts 26:16).

Here the Apostle Paul skillfully recounts his experience on the Damascus road the day that he was saved. Many have overlooked the fact that Paul's conversion launched the *heavenly ministry* of Christ. This is why in Verse 16 the Holy Spirit reveals to us that the apostle was to be a witness both of those things he had seen and of those things in which the Lord would appear unto him.

What did Saul of Tarsus see and hear that memorable day? The nature of the event was such that Paul *looked up* when he heard the voice of the One he had been persecuting. And what did the apostle-to-be behold? He beheld the glorified, resurrected Christ in indescribable glory speaking to him from above! Hence, his words to King Agrippa now take on a new meaning: *"Whereupon, O King Agrippa, I was not disobedient unto the heavenly vision."* From this point forward the Lord was to reveal His heavenly ministry for the Body of Christ through Paul's ministry. Thus, the commands of Christ for the Church of this dispensation are found exclusively in his epistles (I Cor. 14:37).

> "Which He wrought in Christ, when He raised Him from the dead, and set Him at his own right hand in the heavenly places . . . and gave Him to be the head over all things to the Church, which is His Body, the fulness of Him that filleth all in all" (Eph. 1:20-23).

In the Book of Ephesians Paul brings us to the very *summit* of the heavenly ministry of Christ. Since the apostle had been caught up to the third heaven he was well equipped to speak of the following authoritatively. According to the above passage Christ holds an exalted position, being seated at the Father's right hand. This shows favor, for the priest in the Old Testament always approached the altar from the right. In prophecy, after the ascension, Christ is depicted as being seated at the Father's right hand as the *Judge* of all the earth. But here in Ephesians He is portrayed as the *God of all grace,* not willing that any should perish. Thus, salvation is a free gift bestowed upon all who believe that Christ died for their sins and rose again.

Everything about the Body of Christ revolves around the heavenlies. We have been seated with Christ in the heavens. We are *"blessed with all spiritual blessings in the heavenlies."* The spiritual warfare we are said to be engaged in is also being fought in heavenly places. And thanks be unto God, our hope is to one day be with Christ in heaven.

AN ENLIGHTENING CONTRAST

The earthly and heavenly ministries of Christ can best be distinguished by *contrasting* the Rapture, which pertains to us, and the Second Coming of Christ, Israel's hope. The Rapture of the Church is a heavenly event that will bring the age of Grace to its consummation. The following are some of the outstanding features of the Rapture:[2]

A. OUR BLESSED HOPE

First of all, the *Secret Coming of Christ,* as we like to call it, was kept *secret* from the foundation of the world. This glorious event was first revealed to Paul and therefore it is only taught in his epistles (Rom. 16:25 cf. I Cor. 15:51).

Secondly, there are *positively* no signs, times or seasons which will precede this long awaited event. We should mention that this return for the Church which is His Body is *imminent,* which simply means it could take place at any moment (I Thess. 1:10; 4:13-18).

Thirdly, Christ will not come to earth, for those who are alive and remain are said to be *caught up* from the earth along with those in the secret resurrection. Only believers will behold the glory of His presence. (I Thess. 4:16,17; I Cor. 15:51).

Fourthly, this major event is brought to a culmination by the Judgment Seat of Christ, which will transpire in the air as we read in I Thes. 4:17. As to the Judgment Seat of Christ, God is a generous Rewarder, not only "slow to anger but plenteous in mercy" (Rom. 14:10-12; Ps. 103:8-12).

---

2. See page 90

Paul closes the fourth chapter of I Thessalonians by saying, *"Comfort one another with these words."* This phrase should bring a lasting peace to our hearts for we are promised deliverance from the wrath of God to come. The heavenly ministry of Christ, then, will find its *fulfillment* in the *Secret Coming of Christ.*

B. THE SECOND COMING OF CHRIST

Following the same number order, we will now contrast the foregoing section with our Lord's coming spoken of in His earthly ministry:

First and foremost, the *Second Coming of Christ* at the end of the great tribulation has been *made known* since the foundation of the world. Jude sheds some light on this when he writes, "And Enoch also, the seventh from Adam, prophesied of these, saying, Behold, the Lord cometh with ten thousands of His saints." In the *beginning* when men lived to great ages, Enoch *prophesied* that the Lord would return to the earth to execute judgment upon all those who are ungodly.

Secondly, the Messiah's *Second Coming* is *associated* with signs, times and seasons. Few will dispute this well-documented fact. We know, for example, that the sun will be darkened and the moon will be turned to blood. Those believers who survive the horrors of the tribulation will probably be able to calculate the time of the *Second Advent* down to within a few weeks or perhaps even days. We even know that this event will take place during one of the *night* watches in Jerusalem (Study Matt. 24:27-31; 25:1-13; Luke 12:35-40; Acts 2:17-21).

Thirdly, the soles of Messiah's feet will literally *stand*

on the Mount of Olives as He engages the forces of the Anti-Christ in warfare. Unlike the Rapture, in the *Second Coming* both believers and unbelievers shall see Him. "Behold, He cometh with clouds and EVERY EYE shall see Him. . . ." Then shall all the ". . . *tribes of the earth mourn because of Him*" (Zech 14:4; Matt. 24:30; Rev. 1:7).

Fourthly, little wonder the gospel writers instruct their hearers to watch and wait. When the Son of Man returns in glory Israel's hope will give way to reality with the commencement of the millennial kingdom. Christ will rule and reign in righteousness as He judges Israel and the nations (Matt. 25:14-46).

If we understand the distinction between the two ministries of Christ it provides a safeguard against being led astray into a mid, prewrath or post tribulational view of the Rapture. God's plans and purposes for the Body of Christ must *first* be brought to completion before He will resume the Prophetic program.

The reason more have not seen this blessed revelation is because it has been buried beneath the rubble of the traditions and commandments of men. Dear reader, settle it in your mind once and for all to stand up and be numbered for Paul's gospel. Literally thousands are searching for the truth. May God use us as His instruments to commit this message to those who long for a fuller knowledge of His will. AMEN!

THE TWO COMINGS OF CHRIST

Earthly Ministry of Christ	Heavenly Ministry	**Rapture**		Fulfillment of Earthly Ministry of Christ	
Promises His return to the earth and warns of the future Tribulation	Promises His return in the air and only pertains to the Body of Christ.		7 Years Tribulation	2nd Coming of Christ to the earth	1000 yrs. Kingdom on earth
Prophetic Program	**The Mystery**			**Prophetic Program Cont'd**	

7
The Body of Christ

> "Endeavouring to keep the unity of the Spirit in the bond of peace. There is one body, and one Spirit, even as ye are called in one hope of your calling; one Lord, one faith, one baptism, one God and Father of all, who is above all, and through all, and in you all."
> —*Ephesians 4:3-6*

The foregoing *Constitution of Grace* contains seven foundational truths upon which our faith rests. This sevenfold unity of the Spirit, as it is sometimes called, is the binding force which *should* knit our hearts together in the bond of peace. Before we proceed further, there are two significant details about the *unity of the Spirit* which must never be overlooked. First of all, this body of truth was conceived by the Holy Spirit without the assistance of a denominational hierarchy. Secondly, all expressions of doctrinal position for the age of Grace must be in full accordance with this outline of the Spirit.

Beloved, if there is ever to be *doctrinal unity* among the brethren, these instructions of the Spirit must be heeded without reservation. Sadly, many have confused *union* with *unity*. In the minds of some believers, joining with the mainstream of Christendom, even though it may involve compromise, brings a sense of acceptance and security. They reason that if so many people are following a given teaching it must surely be right. Such rationalization is extremely dangerous, especially in view of the fact that just the *opposite* is normally true.

Back in the days preceding Christopher Columbus the world believed that the earth was flat. Only a few courageous men even dared to challenge this ideology. Who was right? Furthermore, some eastern religions boast staggering numbers who follow their mystical persuasions. Are they correct? Even in Biblical times when our Lord dwelt among us, literally hundreds of thousands were saved, but only 120 saw the necessity to obey His command to tarry at Jerusalem until the arrival of the Holy Spirit. In the family of God those who have been the custodians of the truth have always been in the *minority,* and today is no exception.

So then, those who desire to obey God's will in the administration of Grace must acknowledge the sevenfold unity of the Spirit. Unity means *oneness,* not togetherness. And oneness is the true characteristic of those who submit themselves to these seven wonders of grace. Let us never be guilty of sacrificing the faith upon the altar of compromise simply to avoid the criticism of men. May God help us to STAND! *"For our light affliction, which is but for a moment, worketh for us a far more exceeding and eternal weight of glory"* (II Cor. 4:17).

A DISTINCTION THAT MATTERS

"There is one body. . ." (Eph. 4:4).

This, of course, is the first of the seven unities that the Apostle Paul etches upon the human heart. God's principal goal in Paul's epistles is that the Gentiles might abound in the knowledge of the *Mystery.* This is why the

The Body of Christ

apostle teaches us in the Book of Philippians that we should have an understanding of the *things that differ.* Take, for example, the difference between the nation Israel and the Body of Christ. These are two entirely distinct entities which must never be confused. Perhaps the easiest way to distinguish between them is to remember that when you turn to the Prophetic Scriptures, *Israel* reigns supreme. On the other hand, in Paul's epistles the *Body of Christ* is predominant. Let's put this observation to the Berean test to see if it will hold up under the scrutiny of Holy Scripture.

1. ISRAEL IN PROPHECY

"And, behold, a woman of Canaan came out of the same coasts, and cried unto Him, saying, Have mercy on me, O Lord, thou Son of David; my daughter is grievously vexed with a devil. But He answered her not a word. And His disciples came and besought Him, saying, Send her away; for she crieth after us. But He answered and said, I am not sent but unto the lost sheep of the house of Israel" (Matt. 15:22-24).

In time past, God chose Abraham to be the father of the Jews. He promised that through Abraham's seed would come forth a great nation, which we now know to be *Israel.* She was the apple of God's eye and to her *alone* was given the adoption, the glory, the covenants, the giving of the Law, the service of God and the promises. Israel is a *miracle* nation. She was conceived in a miracle (Abraham and Sarah were far beyond the years of childbearing), preserved miraculously and awaits a miraculous deliverance in the future. We need to be well aware that under the old economy she also held a position of *preemi-*

nence far above all the Gentile nations of the world. God channeled *all* of His choicest blessings through her, which eventually were to filter down to the other nations. The hopeless condition of the Gentiles is sketched out for us in Eph. 2:11,12:

> "Wherefore remember, that ye being in time past Gentiles in the flesh. . . . That at that time ye were without Christ, being aliens from the commonwealth of Israel, and strangers from the covenants of promise, having no hope, and without God in the world."

By comparing Matthew with Mark's Gospel we are able to safely conclude that the woman spoken of here in Matt. 15:22 was a Syrophenician who lived in Canaan. In other words, she was a *Gentile* who was without hope and without God in this world. But she had undoubtedly heard of the wonderful works of our Lord and sought Him to have mercy upon her because her daughter was possessed of a demon. And what was our Lord's response to her request? *"He answered her not a word."* He would not even speak to her!

There were also other occasions when our Lord would not give the Gentiles the time of day (John 12:20-23). But the Syrophenician woman was quite persistent; somehow she had to have an audience with the Master! So, she began to follow the disciples around requesting of them that they intercede on her behalf. Nearing the point of exasperation the disciples asked the Lord to send her away. *This woman is troubling us!* Lord, heal her daughter, anything, so she will leave us alone! But He answered His disciples, *"I am not sent but unto the lost sheep of the house of Israel."*

The Body of Christ

Then the woman came and worshipped Him, begging the Master to make her daughter, whom she loved dearly, whole again. But our Lord was adamant: *"It is not meet [fit] to take the children's bread and cast it to the dogs."* This is another way of saying: Is it proper to take the physical and spiritual blessings that rightfully belong to Israel and cast them to a Gentile who is nothing more than a *dog?* Needless to say, these are strong words. Notice, however, this Gentile woman's response: *"Truth, Lord: yet the dogs eat of the crumbs which fall from their masters' table."* This woman was willing to accept any of the blessings that fell from Israel's table. She knew God's blessing was upon the chosen nation and if she was to be saved and her daughter healed she must submit herself to this truth.

Touched by the woman's faith and willingness to subject herself to God's plans and purposes, our Lord had compassion on her and healed her daughter. From this portion, and the Prophetic Scriptures as a whole, we learn the following:

1. Christ is the King of Israel *(Thou Son of David*—vs. 22).

2. Israel is given supremacy over the nations (vs. 24).

3. The Gentiles are to be blessed through Israel (vs. 27,28)

4. Israel, on the earth, was primarily blessed with physical blessings (vs. 28).

2. THE BODY OF CHRIST

As we have seen, in time past the Gentiles were strangers and foreigners to the blessings of God. Bringing our thoughts back to Eph. 2:13 for a moment, it is imperative that we take note of the key phrase, *"But now."* These words indicate that a great *dispensational change* has taken place. Permit me to add a brief commentary as we read this passage together. "But now [in the age of Grace] in Christ Jesus YE [i.e. you Gentiles] who sometimes were far off are made nigh [or have full access unto God] by the blood of Christ."

In the dispensation of Grace Israel no longer holds a position of prominence over the nations. Today, God is saving individuals out of *all* nations to the praise of His glory. Surely, the Scriptures and experience confirm the accuracy of this conclusion. Did any of our readers have to submit themselves to Israel and the Law of Moses to be saved? The Syrophenician woman most certainly did.

When we heard the proclamation of the gospel, how that Christ died for our sins and rose again, we simply believed and were saved. *Grace* rescued us from the cruel taskmaster of sin. The moment we took Christ as our personal Savior the Holy Spirit instantaneously baptized us into the *Body of Christ.*

> "Therefore if any man be in Christ, he is a new creature: old things are passed away; behold, all things are become new" (II Cor. 5:17).

Generally this passage is used to explain how the believer has new life in Christ. The old sinful desires have passed away and now are replaced with a desire to walk in the newness of life. The transformed life is, indeed, taught in the Pauline revelation. However, in the passage under consideration the Apostle Paul does not have the Christian life in view. Rather he is expounding

The Body of Christ

the virtues of the *New Creation.* He begins with the word *"therefore,"* which indicates that we must contemplate what goes there before.

Since the apostle has already concluded in verses 14 and 15 that Christ died for "all," he goes on to say in verse 16, "wherefore henceforth [or from now on], we know no man [whether *Jew or Gentile*], after the flesh." Thus, God has removed the barrier of the Law, making it possible for all men out of every nation to be saved by the Cross. *". . . yea, though we have known Christ after the flesh, yet now henceforth know we HIM no more."* Notice how the tense of the verb in the first part of this sentence is *past present.* We *no longer* know Christ as the lowly Jesus who went about Palestine healing the sick and raising the dead. Nor do we know Him as the King of Kings who will one day sit on the throne of David in the millennial kingdom.

We have come to know Christ in a completely different sense than our predecessors. Today, He is the Lord of glory who has undertaken a new position as the Head of the Church, the Body of Christ (Col. 1:18). Therefore, in verse 17 *"if any man"* (i.e. Jew or Gentile) be in Christ he is a part of the *New Creation.* The New Creation then, is the *Body of Christ.* God is reconciling both Jews and Gentiles, without distinction, in one Body by the blood of the Cross. Furthermore, *"old things are passed away,"* which is to be understood to mean that we are no longer in bondage to the precepts of the Law with its sacrificial system, sabbaths and baptisms.

"Behold all things are become new." As members of His Body we are under *grace,* and accordingly enjoy a new relationship with Christ. The New Creation has the privi-

lege of being blessed with all spiritual blessings in the heavenlies, where our Savior reigns over all and we are said to be seated with Him (Eph. 2:6).

In summary, as we have seen, the first plank of the seven-fold unity of the Spirit is the unique character of the Body of Christ. Thus, the following truths are confined *solely* to the epistles of St. Paul:

1. Christ is the Head of the Body or the *New Creation*.
2. Jews and Gentiles are placed on the same level.
3. The Gentiles are blessed in spite of Israel.
4. The primary blessings of the Body are spiritual.

We've all heard the old adage from down on the farm, "Never put all your eggs into one basket." Well, the same applies to dispensing the written revelation of God. We must distinguish the nation Israel from the Body of Christ, just as we distinguish the brown eggs from the white. Then, they must be *carefully* placed into the *proper* baskets, otherwise, you may end up with scrambled eggs.

To read many commentators, this is exactly what has happened in their careless handling of the Scriptures. They have scrambled the two programs of God. Consequently, many dear saints are confused and frustrated in their study of the greatest story every told.

BEING IN CHRIST

"Salute Andronicus and Junia, my kinsmen, and my fellowprisoners, who are of note among the apostles, who also were *in Christ* before me" (Rom. 16:7).

The Body of Christ

About the time we begin to strengthen our grip on the truth, a passage such as the above comes along, causing us to have dispensational nightmares. To complicate matters even further, we can be sure as the cows will come home, that someone is going to question us as to how any could have been *in Christ* before Paul, if he was the first member of the Body of Christ.

There are some questions, of course, that we are unable to answer; therefore, it may be the better part of wisdom to wait for further light from God. Those who attempt to respond to inquiries where they lack knowledge are like the man who tries to walk on quicksand—*sunk!* Thankfully, the Spirit of God has graciously given us many helpful insights on this very perplexing Scripture passage, that we might have a fuller appreciation of the manifold wisdom of God.

IN CHRIST REDEMPTIVELY

When the Apostle Paul makes reference to those who were *in Christ* before him he does not mean to imply that Andronicus and Junia were in the *Body of Christ* before him. It deserves our most thoughtful attention that the Church, the Body of Christ, was not even introduced on the stage of this world until the conversion of Paul, who was the *first* member of that Body (Col. 1:24-26; I Tim. 1:12-16). The phrase *in Christ* used by the Apostle here in Rom. 16:7 is to be understood in its broadest sense of *redemption*. Every blood-washed saint of *all* ages can be said to be *in Christ* redemptively. He stands before God, not in himself, but *in Christ!* The Holy Spirit effectively conveys this truth to us in the form of a *type* from the days of Noah. We should pause here to add that a *type* has

99

been defined as being "a divine illustration of some truth."

Keeping in mind that the Scriptures are spiritually discerned, who could fail to see that the ark of Noah was a type of Christ? For 120 years Noah, who was a preacher of righteousness, warned the people of his day to escape the judgment to come by believing God, which meant they had to enter into the security of the ark. As the storm clouds gathered the Lord said unto Noah, "Come thou and all thy house *into* the ark . . . and Noah went *in,* and his sons, and his wife, and his sons' wives with him, *into the ark,* because of the waters of the flood . . . and the Lord shut him *in"* (Gen. 7:1,7,16).

With Noah and his family safely tucked away in the ark, the skies began to turn black, changing the laughter of men into paralyzing fear. As with most major storms, probably an eerie calm fell over the earth. Then, without notice, God suddenly unleashed His wrath by opening the windows of heaven and breaking up the subterranean waters of the deep, resulting in the *universal* flood. All the ungodly who were outside the ark were consumed in terror as they were swept away in judgment. The story of Noah and the ark is a beautiful picture of the child of God being *in Christ* redemptively, which teaches us that *all* believers are beyond the reach of judgment on the basis of Christ's shed blood.

PETER'S HELPING HAND

"Which sometime were disobedient, when once the longsuffering of God waited in the days of Noah, while the ark was a-preparing, wherein few, that is, eight souls were saved by water.

The Body of Christ

"The like figure whereunto even baptism doth also now save us (not the putting away of the filth of the flesh, but the answer of a good conscience toward God,) by the resurrection of Jesus Christ" (I Pet. 3:20,21).

Peter lends us a helping hand on the subject of redemption when he too refers back to the days of Noah to reveal that there were 8 souls saved through the water or through the judgment. He goes on to add, "whereunto even baptism doth also now save us." In other words, the *ark of Noah* and *baptism* are corresponding truths, which set forth the believer's redemption in Christ.

But which *baptism* is Peter referring to here? We must never lose sight of the fact that there are 12 different baptisms taught in the Word of God. This baptism certainly could *not* be a water ceremony. If it is, then water baptism saves, and even our Baptist friends do not draw this conclusion. We believe the answer is found in our Lord's own words in Luke 12:50: *"But I have a baptism to be baptized with; and how am I straitened till it be accomplished."*

These words were spoken by our Lord well into His earthly ministry. When He spoke about having "a baptism to be baptized with," He was teaching His disciples about His impending death on the Cross. If we understand that the term "baptism" means "full identification," then we see that Christ was *identified* with death in order to be the Redeemer of mankind.

Returning to I Pet. 3:21, it is Christ's *identification* with death that saves men in any dispensation, though this was not revealed until Paul (Rom. 3:21,25). As members of the Body of Christ we share this in common with the nation Israel—this being one of the connections between Prophecy and the Mystery. Subsequently, no matter under which dispensation a sinner is saved, he is saved *on the basis* of the blood that flowed freely at Calvary's Cross. It was there that Christ gave Himself as a ransom for the sins of the world, which was to be "manifested in due time" through Paul's gospel (I Tim. 2:5-7). Furthermore, it is on the grounds of Christ's finished work that we are able to have a good conscience toward God. This dovetails perfectly with what Paul states in the Book of Hebrews: *"How much more shall the blood of Christ, who through the eternal Spirit offered Himself without spot to God, purge your conscience from dead works to serve the living God?"* (Heb. 9:14).

Peter is careful to state that a man is *not* saved, *nor* can he ever expect to have a good conscience toward God, by the "putting away of the filth of the flesh." As we already know the "putting away of the filth of the flesh" is done by washing with water in order to cleanse. He is informing his hearers that it is Christ's death baptism that saves them, not water baptism, which was merely the shadow.

DISPENSATIONALLY IN CHRIST

"Paul, an apostle of Jesus Christ by the will of God, to the saints which are at Ephesus, and to the faithful in Christ Jesus.

"Blessed be the God and Father of our Lord Jesus Christ, who hath blessed us with all spiritual blessings in heavenly places in Christ" (Eph. 1:1,3).

Here we have another matter entirely. Paul uses the phrase *in Christ* in these passages in a completely different sense than he did back in the Book of Romans. As the

The Body of Christ

apostle begins to unfold the spiritual blessings that we enjoy in Christ, he purposely limits the phrase to the Church, the Body of Christ. This is an important dispensational distinction which must not be overlooked. *Only* believers, during this dispensation of Grace, can be said to be *in Christ,* as far as being in the Body of Christ is concerned. The company of saints who make up Christ's Body consist of *only* those who are saved from the conversion of the Apostle Paul until the sound of the trump at the Rapture (I Tim. 1:15,16; I Cor. 12:27; I Thess. 4:13-18). *Only* those who have been saved under the terms of salvation found in Paul's epistles make up the true church of this dispensation (I Cor. 15:1-4).

The Holy Spirit does a marvelous work on our behalf the moment we are saved, when He takes us out of Adam and places us into Christ, thus identifying us with His death, burial and resurrection. We are not a part of the noisy machinery of an organization; instead we have literally become members of a living organism, joined to other members. Christ is the Head of this Body, who not only gives it life, but also direction and purpose.

> "For by one Spirit are we *all* baptized into one body, whether we be Jews or Gentiles, whether we be bond or free; and have been *all* made to drink into one Spirit" (I Cor. 12:13).

This spiritual baptism by the Spirit pertains directly to us and stresses the oneness that we enjoy as a result of being joined to the Body. It is important to note that the emphasis of this passage is on the word "all." We are *all* baptized by the same Spirit. *All* are indwelt by the same Spirit. *All* members of the Body have spiritual

103

life, because *all* have been made to drink into one Spirit. This is why believers rejoice *together* when a sinner trusts Christ as his or her personal Savior. On the other hand, when a good friend who is a fellow-believer is taken in death, we *share* in the sadness with the family.

"For the body is not one member, but many. If the foot shall say, Because I am not the hand, I am not of the body; is it therefore not of the body?" (I Cor. 12:14,15).

"But now hath God set the members every one of them in the Body, as it hath pleased Him" (I Cor. 12:18).

God in His sovereignty places each of the members in the Body as it pleases Him. Reading on here in Chapter 12 we learn that the Corinthians were not timid in expressing their discontent with their placement in the Body. Apparently many of them were disgruntled, desiring rather to have a more visible position like the apostle held. Their reasoning was reprehensible, when we take into consideration that if all in the congregation were pastors, who would take the offering or sing or play the piano or usher, or even more importantly *listen* to the preaching of the Word?

God in His infinite wisdom has placed each member in the Body where we will be the most useful and productive. If every member of the true Church upheld his God-given responsibility it would undoubtedly have a more profound impact than this world has ever known. Those saints who were shut away in hidden places praying for the Apostle Paul's ministry seemed so insignificant to the Corinthians. Little did they realize that the fruits of his labors were oftentimes a direct result of the prayers of these so-called "silent saints."

The Body of Christ

It is our conviction that because we are members of Christ's Body we all have an obligation to treat one another with the utmost respect. We may not see eye to eye on every minor doctrine or dot our i's or cross our t's the same way, but this does not give us the liberty to deal with our brothers and sisters *in Christ* in an ungracious manner. This does not mean, though, that we should be remiss concerning our responsibility to point out unsound doctrine. What it does mean is that we are not to be ungracious when doing so. It should be our heart's desire to recognize fully the oneness of the Body, just as we do with the members of our own natural body. Let us follow the example of Paul when he says: "Brethren, if a man be overtaken in a fault, ye which are spiritual, restore such an one in the spirit of meekness; considering thyself, lest thou also be tempted" (Gal. 6:1).

The believers of this dispensation have the unique honor to not only be *in Christ* redemptively, but also *in Christ* as far as being in the Body of Christ is concerned. Christ, who is our Head, is the one we share in common—He is the common denominator.

8
The One Spirit

"Endeavoring to keep the unity of the Spirit in the bond of peace. There is one body, and one Spirit, even as ye are called in one hope of your calling."
—*Ephesians 4:3,4*

The second "unity" delivered to us by the Apostle Paul is the glorious truth that there is *one Spirit*. Needless to say, the subject of the Holy Spirit has taken center stage over the past two or three decades. This is due in part to the rise of the present day Charismatic Movement, which emphasizes the need to "return to Pentecost" with its *miraculous* manifestations of the Spirit. While to some degree they are Scripturally correct, they are dispensationally wrong—dead wrong! Here again we must rightly divide the Word of truth, for the ministry of the Holy Spirit has changed dramatically with the unveiling of the revelation of the Mystery. Thus, the person of the Spirit is not under consideration as much as His *administration* when Paul uses the above phrase. However, since there are so many uncertain trumpets being sounded these days about the person of the Holy Spirit, perhaps this is the best place to commence our study.

THE COMFORTER

"And I will pray the Father, and He shall give you another Comforter, that He may abide with you forever" (John 14:16).

As we read from the final chapter of our Lord's life we

The One Spirit

learn that He gathered His disciples together in the upper room to prepare them for His departure by way of the Cross. Perceiving that they were deeply troubled by His words, the Master promised them that in His absence He would give them *another* Comforter. Consulting the original language, the term "another" is used in two senses in the Word of God. First, we have "another" (Gr. *Heteros*) of a "different sort." For example, if I pick up an orange in one hand and someone hands me an apple in my other hand, both are fruit, but the apple is a fruit of another or *different* kind. However, if I place the apple down and pick up another (Gr. *Allos*) orange, I am now holding two pieces of fruit which are the *same* kind.

Our Lord uses the latter term *Allos* here in John 14 to convey to His disciples that He would send them *another* Comforter of the *same kind,* who would teach them and bring all things to remembrance (John 14:26). These parting instructions undeniably confirm that the Spirit of God is a *person* who possesses personality, which essentially means that He has an *intellect, emotions* and a *will.*

Intellect: According to I Corinthians 2:10-12 the Holy Spirit is said to have knowledge, in that He knows and searches the deep things of God. Subsequently, He is the one who imparted the will of God to those who penned the *original manuscripts* of the Scriptures, which incidentally eliminated the possibility of error.

Emotions: The Spirit also has emotions, for we are instructed by the Apostle Paul to ". . . *grieve not the Holy Spirit"* in Ephesians 4:30. But this is precisely what takes place when the believer allows sin to have dominion over him.

Will: Finally, the Spirit of God dispenses spiritual gifts to all members of the Body of Christ, ". . . *severally as He wills"* (I Cor. 12:11). Choice is an act of the will.

So then, the Holy Spirit is not merely a force as some would have us believe. He is a real person, which justifies the Scripture's frequent usage of personal pronouns such as: He, His, Him, etc. "Even the Spirit of truth; Whom the world cannot receive, because it seeth HIM not, neither knoweth HIM: but ye know HIM; for HE dwelleth with you, and shall be in you" (John 14:17).

As mentioned earlier, the apostle assumes we are already acquainted with the person of the Holy Spirit. Therefore, his primary motivation in making reference to the *one Spirit* is to point out that a major dispensational change has taken place in the work of the Spirit. It is important then to carefully distinguish between the role of the Holy Spirit under the kingdom gospel and His role under the gospel of the grace of God.

THE KINGDOM GOSPEL AND THE SPIRIT

"And, being assembled together with them, commanded them that they should not depart from Jerusalem, but wait for the promise of the Father, which, saith He, ye have heard of me" (Acts 1:4).

Incredibly, many have failed to see that the things recorded in the early chapters of Acts are simply a *continuation* of the earthly ministry of Christ. As a matter of fact, many of the promises our Lord made to His kinsmen after the flesh were literally fulfilled in the early Acts period.

Prior to our Lord's ascension He instructed His disciples

The One Spirit

to remain in Jerusalem that they might receive the promise of the Father which, of course, was the coming Holy Spirit. We glean from verse 5 that the believers at that time were promised to be baptized *with* the Holy Spirit. According to Mark's gospel we are told that Christ would be the *baptizer* who would officially identify them with the Spirit on the day of Pentecost.

"I [John] indeed have baptized you with water: but He [Christ] shall baptize you with the Holy Spirit (Mark 1:8).

The purpose of this baptism is found in Acts 1:8 where we read: *"But ye shall receive power, after that the Holy Spirit is come upon you: and ye shall be witnesses unto me both in Jerusalem, and in all Judaea. . . ."* The significance of this event was to empower them with supernatural sign gifts that they might more effectively testify of the resurrection of Christ. To be identified with the Spirit in this manner meant that the recipient would be able to speak in tongues, heal the sick and raise the dead.

In Acts chapter 2 we have a very graphic description of the arrival of the Holy Spirit:

"And when the day of Pentecost was fully come, they were all with one accord in one place. . . . And they were all filled with the Holy Spirit, and began to speak with other tongues, as the Spirit gave them utterance" (Acts 2:1,4).

The day of Pentecost that is spoken of here was a *Jewish* feast day and has absolutely nothing to do with the Gentiles or the Church, the Body of Christ. Pentecost means 50th, because it followed 50 days after the feast of firstfruits according to the Law of the Lord given to Israel

(Lev. 23:1-10). Three of the seven Levitical feasts were national holidays, when all Israelites were required to make a pilgrimage back to Jerusalem to offer specific blood sacrifices and rekindle the national spirit. It was during the feast of Pentecost that Christ baptized His 120 Jewish followers with the Holy Spirit. This wonderfully prepared them to announce to the religious leaders in Israel that they were being given a *second chance*. If Israel nationally would have simply repented of crucifying their Messiah then God would have sent the times of refreshing (millennial kingdom) (Acts 3:14-21).

When Christ baptized these believers, who indeed were the true Pentecostal believers, they were *all* filled with the Holy Spirit. With regard to Acts 2:4 we should thoughtfully note the phrase "*. . . they were all filled. . . .*" It is evident from the context which follows that the Spirit of God took *complete control* of their lives, including supplying their every need. Consequently, they were to sell their homes and their possessions and have all things in common (Acts 2:44,45; 4:32-37).

Another benefit of this filling was that they were given the gift of tongues (known languages) as the Spirit gave them utterance. Beloved ones, God's timing is always perfect! The day of Pentecost afforded the 120 in the upper room the opportunity to address their countrymen who had gathered in Jerusalem to observe the feast. Thus, the "little flock" was able to communicate in *other languages* all that had transpired in Jerusalem concerning the Messiah. Bear in mind, that many of these Israelites were from other countries and did not speak the mother tongue.[1]

---

1. Hebrew language

The One Spirit

Since we have sufficiently nailed down the ministry of the Holy Spirit in Prophecy, we now want to turn to the Mystery program where we are in for a pleasant surprise!

THE MYSTERY AND THE SPIRIT

"For by one Spirit are we all baptized into one Body, whether we be Jews or Gentiles, whether we be bond or free; and have been all made to drink into one Spirit" (I Cor. 12:13).

In the dispensation of Grace the ministry of the Holy Spirit has changed significantly. Through a special revelation the Apostle Paul announces a *new baptism* which is performed by the operation of the Spirit. This is the one baptism referred to in Eph. 4:5, which explains why we do not advocate a second work of grace.

Today it is the Spirit of God who is the baptizer, as our passage clearly stipulates. According to Paul's words here to the Corinthians, the purpose of this baptism is to spiritually baptize or *identify* us with Christ's Body, whether we be Jews or Gentiles. Furthermore, we are said to be identified with Christ's death, burial and resurrection. As only God could see, our old man was crucified with Christ. Since we do not bury someone who is yet alive, we have the assurance that our old man is dead, inasmuch as he has been crucified and buried with Christ. And wonder of wonders, our new man has been risen with Christ to walk in newness of life (Rom. 6:3,4). Shall we then permit sin to have dominion over us? God forbid! As the apostle says: *"Let not sin therefore reign in your mortal body...."* Rather we should seek to *"...be filled with the Spirit."*

"And be not drunk with wine, wherein is excess; but be filled with the Spirit" (Eph. 5:18).

Could there be a more solemn admonition of danger? Paul warns the saints at Ephesus not to be drunk with wine, wherein is excess. Apparently there were some in this assembly who had overindulged themselves in strong drink. Such carelessness was destroying their testimony as well as casting a poor reflection on the cause of Christ.

One who is drunk with wine is under the influence of a substance that has brought nothing but heartache to those who partake. Strong drink affects the body in adverse ways, oftentimes impairing judgment and causing one's speech to be slurred. Balance is also disrupted, resulting in one stumbling about. It is a pathetic sight to say the least, but the point is, that wine takes charge of the *whole* person. Paul's argument is, don't allow wine to control you, but rather allow the Spirit to have control of your life. In this regard, it should be noted that the apostle does not say "We are all filled with the Spirit" as stated in Acts 2:4. Instead, he challenges us "... *but be filled with the Spirit,*" just as a subject might fill one's mind.

Many have misunderstood Paul's words here in Ephesians, reasoning that the *filling of the Spirit* has to do with having more of the Spirit. Actually, we are already indwelt by the Spirit, but He can and should have more of us. This is accomplished by yielding ourselves to the control of the Spirit, and our members as instruments of righteousness. It means casting down prideful self and no longer having things our way. Rather, we must learn the necessity of bringing into captivity every thought to the obedience of Christ.

In addition to this, the Word of God must have a preeminent place in our lives. Every child of God must give himself daily to meditating on the Scriptures, for they will provide a sure foundation upon which to rest his faith. We should be diligently comparing Scripture with Scripture, seeking to understand the sense that is given. Mark these words and mark them well, the dividends are most rewarding!

Prayer must become second nature to us as well. As natural as it is for us to breathe without giving it a thought, this is how natural it should be for us to go to our Heavenly Father in prayer. One of the reasons the spiritual lives of believers are so anemic revolves around the fact that we have stopped taking everything to God in prayer.

The Holy Spirit's influence should affect every area of our life, resulting in a remarkable transformation in our attitudes, actions and desires. Thus our conduct should be above reproach, avoiding even the appearance of evil. If these practical strands of truth are implemented in the Christian experience, they will ensure everlasting blessing.

The filling of the Spirit, then, is something we must attain to by *grace* through *faith*. Furthermore, the Spirit-centered life today will *never* manifest itself with miracles, signs and wonders. Someone may be thinking: But why did God use supernatural gifts to introduce His plans and purposes for the Body of Christ? The answer is twofold: First and foremost, they were a *sign* to Israel that God was withdrawing His blessing from the chosen nation that He might turn to the *Gentiles.* Secondly, Paul's new apostolic office had to be confirmed with miracles and wonders, thereby announcing to the world God was initiating a *New Creation* that had been kept secret from ages and generations past. With the maturing of the age of Grace the signs of the Acts period gradually were discontinued. Now *abides* something far better—Faith, Hope and Love.

RESULTS OF THE SPIRIT-CENTERED LIFE

We have established that the Spirit-centered life today will *not* manifest itself in a "tongues" experience, thus making one incoherent. Nor are signs and wonders to be expected or sought after, for these were the results of the "filling with the Spirit" under the kingdom gospel (Acts 2:1-10). Paul's gospel reveals that the characteristics of the Spirit's direction today are *joy, thankfulness,* and *submission* (Eph. 5:19-21).

The Spirit's control of the believers life always produces *joy* which springs from a knowledge of God's Word. He will understand what God expects of him and his desire will be to please the Lord by carrying out every aspect of His marching orders. His life becomes like a symphony with each part harmonizing, bringing forth a beautiful melody to the glory of God. He'll have a song in his heart produced from being right with God, that will not go unnoticed by those around him.

The strength of these words were witnessed in the lives of Paul and Silas when they were imprisoned at Philippi (Acts 16:20-25). They had been falsely accused, beaten with rods and thrust into the innermost prison. Prisons back then were dark, damp and oftentimes rat infested. Jeremiah tells us that he was lowered down into the dungeon with cords and sunk into the mire to his knees (Jer. 38:6). If that was not enough to strike fear into one's heart, the fear of starvation was.

The One Spirit

But what's this we hear coming forth from the inner prison at midnight? Is it murmuring or complaints of, "How could God have allowed this?" No, it's Paul and Silas praying and singing praises unto God. Are they dazed from the beating? Quite the contrary, we find them with their hearts overflowing with *joy* to the praise and glory of God. Unquestionably, the joy-bells ringing in their hearts had a profound impact on the other prisoners and ultimately led to the conversion of the Philippian jailer.

How sad though, that we have so many, "songless saints" in these last days of Grace. Remember, there will be *joy* unbounded in the lives of those who lead a Spirit-blessed life.

Another outcome of a Spirit-led life is that we are able to give thanks in *all things*. The spiritually minded man will have a thankful heart and gives thanks to God even through times of adversity. Moreover, he rises above adversity knowing that the peace of God will keep his heart and mind. He will even *thank* God through times of suffering for the honor to suffer for His name's sake. Also, he rejoices for having another opportunity to learn from the hardship that he is now encountering. In a nutshell, he realizes and fully appreciates that God is in control.

Finally, the Spirit-centered life is willing to *submit* to others for the sake of the furtherance of the gospel. Sometimes we need to set our personal differences aside, in order to remove the impasse that is standing in the way of progress. This does not mean we strive for peace at any price or compromise our stand. We should, however, for the sake of unity seek to be a *help* rather than a hindrance to the Lord's work. For the well-being of all, sometimes we must swallow our pride and do what is best for the common cause. A good illustration of this is given to us by Martin Luther:

> "One day two sheep were crossing in the opposite direction on the same path. The way was quite narrow due to the fact that on the left was a deep ravine and on the right was a sharp drop to a large body of water.
>
> "When the sheep came face to face they were unable to pass one another without plunging to their death. Neither were they able to back up without fear of slipping off one of the edges. How do you suppose they solved their dilemma? Interestingly, one of the sheep lay down, allowing the other to walk over its back. This enabled both to pass safely."

IN CLOSING

The Spirit who moved upon the face of the waters on the first day of creation is the *same* Spirit who illuminates us to the wonders of God's grace. But the relationship of the Spirit between the two programs of God differs, as we have shown and as the following outline indicates:

KINGDOM GOSPEL	GRACE GOSPEL
1. The person of the Holy Spirit	1. Same person

2. Baptism *with* the Spirit
   a. Baptizer—Christ
   b. Purpose was to empower Israel with supernatural gifts.
	2. Baptism *by* the Spirit
	   a. Baptizer—Holy Spirit
	   b. Purpose is to identify us with Christ's Body

3. Filled with the Spirit	3. Be filled with the Spirit

9
Identifying Our One Hope

"There is one body, and one Spirit, even as ye are called in one hope of your calling."

—*Ephesians 4:4*

A Christian commentator got my attention a short time ago when he asked: "Have you noticed in our modern day that good news is always approached from a negative standpoint? If Thomas Edison were alive today and had just invented the electric light bulb, can you imagine how this would be reported on the evening news? It probably would go something like this:

'Hello, This is Dan Rather reporting. At the top of the news this evening there is a crisis in the candle industry!! Due to the invention of the light bulb by Edison, hundreds face unemployment, and financial disaster in the candle industry is imminent!'"

This type of negative approach, of course, overshadows the good news, causing it to be neutralized, and creates in society a disposition of indifference. The ways of the world have had a profound effect upon the attitude of Christians. Subsequently, we too have become subject to apathy. God's good news, however, based on His Son, is always presented in an *affirmative* way. In a world that is on the brink of destruction, God extends to the believer a sustaining hope. And though the storms of life may overtake us, *hope,* as we shall see, is the anchor of our soul.

DEFINING THE BIBLICAL WORD "HOPE"

Consulting the *Random House Dictionary,* we discover that in our modern English, *hope* is defined as follows: "The *feeling* that what is desired is also possible, or that events *may* turn out for the best" (emphasis ours). Our English usage of the word *hope* is a "hope-so" hope, denoting an element of doubt or uncertainty. For example, many of us would like to see legislation enacted to eliminate the month of January from the calendar. Here in the Midwest, most of the time you have to use an eight horsepower snowblower to get to the mailbox. Then it normally takes about an hour to build up enough courage to go out and see what the morning mail will bring. With fear gripping your heart, another January day brings the Federal Income Tax, State Income Tax, local taxes, Notice of Assessment, and a natural gas bill that you would think would be large enough to heat the Empire State Building!

Amidst all this gloom and doom there is also the *Publishers' Clearing House* offer to win 10 million dollars with absolutely *no obligation!* Their timing is carefully designed to prey on our misfortune. A ray of hope flashes across the minds of most Americans. Think of it! Enough money to pay all those outstanding debts! Everyone who enters the Sweepstakes has high "hopes" that he will be the big winner. This *hope,* however, is based on nothing more than *wishful* thinking. The odds against winning the *Publishers' Clearing House Sweepstakes* are astronomical. You probably have a better chance of being hit by

Identifying Our One Hope

lightning on a clear day! One thing you can count on with certainty is receiving a bill for all the magazines you have purchased. So then, we use the word "hope" in the sense that by *chance* it may come to pass, but in all *probability* it will not—this is the world's view of HOPE!!

When studying this word in the Scriptures we must be very cautious never to impose our definition from modern English upon the Biblical usage. Therefore, it is important to define the term from the language that was used in the writer's day. Words oftentimes become archaic and may even change their meanings altogether through the centuries. From the Greek language, in which our New Testament was written, *hope* means "confident expectation of something sure, something that will positively take place." This is confirmed in Hebrews 6:19 where the Word of God states, *"Which hope we have as an anchor of the soul, both sure and steadfast. . . ."* When God extends to the believer a *certain* hope we can be *confident* that it will come to pass, based upon the *unchanging* Word of God. He Who has promised is faithful to His Word and cannot lie! (Titus 1:2).

IN SEARCH OF OUR HOPE

Dispensationalists frequently refer to the "one hope" of the Body of Christ in their preaching and teaching (See Eph. 4:4). However, there are many different views as to exactly what is meant by our "one hope." In this respect, one Pastor claims our *hope* is the resurrection! Another holds that it is to inherit eternal life! Still another says we have a blessed hope, which is the Rapture of the Church! Then there are those who insist that we have a *heavenly* hope! Is it possible to reconcile all of these views? Each of the above statements contains some element of truth, but not the *whole* truth! What then, according to the Scriptures, is our *confident expectation* in this dispensation of Grace?

The Apostle Paul emphatically states in Ephesians 4:4 that the Body of Christ is indeed united by *one hope!* "There is one body, and one spirit, even as ye are called in one hope of your calling." Rather than being left to drift on a sea of speculation and the opinions of men, we want to turn to the Scriptures. After all, the best commentary on the Bible is the Bible itself. It is imperative at this point to ask, "What saith the Lord?"

> "Paul, an Apostle of Jesus Christ by the commandment of God our Savior, and Lord Jesus Christ, which is our hope" (I Tim. 1:1).

> "Remembering without ceasing your work of faith, and labour of love, and patience of hope in our Lord Jesus Christ, in the sight of God and our Father" (I Thes. 1:3).

As we seek to define our *one hope* in Ephesians, it becomes very evident from I Timothy 1:1 and I Thessalonians 1:3 that *our hope is centered in Christ* as He is set forth in His heavenly ministry. He is the *object* upon which the believer's hope is fixed. This means, of course, that all other references to this term in the Pauline epistles are to be understood as being merely integral *parts* of our *one hope*. In other words, they are *all* going to converge in some way into the current undertaking of Christ on behalf of the members of His Body. Therefore, believers at this hour can look forward with confident expectation to the future, knowing they will be called into the heavenlies to be with Christ which is far better. We are to understand that only the Lord has the authority to fulfill all the promises given to the Church. Consequently, Christ in His heavenly ministry is the *center* of all aspects of our hope, as briefly expounded under the following headings:

HOPE OF SALVATION

"But let us, who are of the day, be sober, putting on the breastplate of faith and love; and for an helmet, the hope of salvation" (I Thes. 5:8).

Before the collapse of Communism in eastern Europe we read a UPI report about the daring escape of a handful of East Germans who fled to West Germany. The East Germans plotted, conspired and gathered materials for months to construct a hot air balloon. When completed, the balloon was inflated and slowly lifted off the ground, heading for a new homeland. They flew out of communist East Germany, over the Berlin Wall amid gunfire, and safely escaped to freedom in West Germany. The story had all the intrigue of a Sherlock Holmes thriller. While escapes from danger and persecution have been numerous throughout history, there is one great escape that will surpass them all. The great escape of which I speak, will be the Church being caught out *before* the tribulation period begins!

The hope of salvation is *the great escape* dimension of our hope. In the above passage, the hope of salvation is *not* referring to salvation from our sins but, rather, deliverance from the wrath of God in the coming Day of the Lord. The context of I Thessalonians 5 clearly points this out. Furthermore, in Verse 5 we read, *"Ye are all the chil-*

dren of light, and the children of the day: we are not of the night, nor of darkness."* The apostle reveals that we are the children of light; that is, we are members of the Body of Christ, who have been saved during God's declaration of grace and peace in this age of Grace. We are the children of the day. This has a relation to the *Day of Christ,* that glorious time of the *Rapture* and Judgment Seat of Christ in heaven (Phil. 1:6).

It also deserves our most thoughtful attention to note that the Apostle Paul emphatically states in Verse 5, ". . . we [the Body of Christ] are not of the night, nor of darkness." This is related to the prophetic night, a time of darkness, which is synonymous with the seven-year tribulation period. As the prophet Zephaniah warns, the Day of the Lord is a day of wrath, a day of darkness, thick darkness, when the mighty men shall cry bitterly (Zeph. 1:14-18). The purpose of this time of darkness in the future tribulation period will be twofold: First it is a time of chastening of the nation Israel to bring her to the Messiah. Second, the nations of the world will be punished for their rejection and rebellion against God's Anointed One (Zech 13:6-9; Ps. 2:1-12).

We must remember in this administration of Grace that we are ambassadors for Christ (II Cor. 5:20). An ambassador is one who represents his nation or ruler in a foreign land. Today believers are representing Christ in His absence here on earth. Incidentally, it is interesting that when one nation declares war against another nation one of the first things that is done is to remove its ambassador to a safe location. This will also be true of the Church. God is going to remove His ambassadors before He

Identifying Our One Hope

declares war upon this sinful world. Thankfully, the Body of Christ will escape this terrible judgment to come.

"For God hath not appointed us [the Body of Christ] to wrath [God's wrath in the future tribulation], but to obtain salvation [deliverance from the tribulation] by our Lord Jesus Christ" (I Thes. 5:9).

Who shall be the one to lead such a gallant escape? We shall obtain deliverance from that dreaded time of Jacob's trouble by *our Lord Jesus Christ* (I Thes. 1:10). Our hope of deliverance rests upon the person of Christ, that He will honor His Word and return to catch us out before the judgment of God is unleashed.

THE HOPE OF RESURRECTION

"If in this life only we have hope in Christ, we are of all men most miserable. But now is Christ risen from the dead, and become the first fruits of them that slept" (I Cor. 15:19,20).

The resurrection is another dimension of our hope, which is Christ. It will be *the method* the Lord is going to use to bring the saints of God into a complete state. Those who die before the time of the Rapture are transported to the third heaven by the angels of God to await the resurrection of their bodies. Indeed, we all await with great anticipation the fulfillment of this aspect of our hope. Once death takes charge, the soul and the spirit depart from the body. Thus, the Scripture is fulfilled, *". . . to be absent from the body, and to be present with the Lord"* (II Cor. 5:8). However, believers in the disembodied state are in an "unclothed" condition, which is another way of saying they are incomplete (II Cor. 5:4). Paul also informs us how the child of God earnestly desires, ". . . to be clothed upon with our house which is from heaven"

(II Cor. 5:2). This, undoubtedly, is a reference to the resurrected, glorified body the saved are going to receive at the Rapture of the Church. Furthermore, it is needful for us to remember the words of our Lord in His earthly ministry when He said in John 11:25, *"I am the resurrection and the life...."* Christ is the Resurrection!

Because Christ has conquered death and risen again He has made our future resurrection certain. But, when will the hope of the resurrection be fulfilled? The answer to this question is, when Christ returns in the Rapture at the close of this dispensation. He will appear in the "air," the upper atmosphere, and with a shout will raise the members of His Body who have died first; then we who are alive and remain will be caught up with them in the clouds and so shall we forever be with the Lord (I Thes. 4:15,16). Without Christ there is no resurrection. Indeed, He is our *hope!*

PAUL, OUR PATTERN

"Be ye followers of me, even as I also am of Christ" (I Cor. 11:1).

"Howbeit for this cause I obtained mercy, that in me first Jesus Christ might shew forth all longsuffering, for a pattern to them which should hereafter believe on Him to life everlasting" (I Tim. 1:16).

What is the purpose of a pattern? A dress designer who is planning a new line of dresses begins his creative design by first making a pattern, which is a diagram or model to be followed in making things. The seamstress takes the pattern and cuts the material following the designated form and, upon sewing it together, produces a finished product. Every dress of the new design will follow the same pattern.

Identifying Our One Hope

If we are to walk well-pleasing unto God we have to follow the life and ministry of the Apostle Paul who is *our pattern*. He was the first one saved into the Body, and his conversion is a demonstration of the longsuffering of God. Wherefore, everyone saved since him is following the original pattern, manifesting the *longsuffering of God* in salvation. The *life* of Paul, then, is an ordained pattern that God has established for the believer to follow during the course of the dispensation of Grace.

Believing this truth to be self-evident, it would only be natural to search the Scriptures to learn what Paul's hope was and follow him in it:

"For to me to live is Christ, and to die is gain" (Phil. 1:21).

"For I am in a strait betwixt two, having a desire to depart, and to be with Christ; which is far better" (Phil. 1:23).

"For our conversation is in heaven; from whence also we look for the Savior, the Lord Jesus Christ" (Phil. 3:20).

To this writer it seems very obvious that the hope of the Apostle Paul was to be with Christ in the heavenlies. How Paul longed to be with his Savior, whom he had so bitterly persecuted, then so faithfully served! To die was *gain* to the Apostle, for he knew that if he lost his life at the hand of the executioner at Rome he would be with Christ, which was far better than living in this sin-cursed world. Have we exhibited this attitude in our Christian life? And if not by death, Paul longed to be with Christ at His appearance from heaven. In both cases his hope was vested in Christ, who would return for the Church and take it home to glory. *Paul's hope was Christ!* If you are following God's pattern, then your hope is also to be with Christ in the heavenlies.

How important is Christ? Without Him we are nothing. Without Him we would have *no hope*. Without Christ there is no heaven, no salvation, no resurrection, no Rapture and no eternal life! Each one of these aspects of our hope is contingent upon the person and work of Christ in His present *heavenly ministry*. HE IS OUR "ONE HOPE!" Believe and be saved; then you will understand the words of the apostle, *"Christ in you, the hope of glory."*

10
One Lord

"There is . . . One Lord, one faith, one baptism."
—*Ephesians 4:5*

The fourth unity of the Spirit brings us to the threshold of another new revelation. We are often admonished as Americans to "Remember Pearl Harbor," but it is also essential to never forget Paul's words to the Corinthians, "I will come to visions and revelations in the Lord." When the apostle singles out the phrase *one Lord* here in Ephesians 4:5 it bears a direct relationship to the dispensation of Grace in which we live. As we search the Pauline epistles as to the significance of this phrase it becomes unmistakably clear that Paul is speaking of *Christ's authority* over the Church, which is His Body.

"Authority" isn't among the most popular subjects in our day and time. Needless to say, the closing words of the Book of Judges seem all too appropriate: *". . . every man did that which was right in his own eyes."* The spirit of lawlessness that presently prevails throughout our land can be summed up in one word—REBELLION! Every time a mother has an abortion it is nothing more than an act of rebellion against God, who is the giver of all life.

Furthermore, it is reported that the top seven discipline problems in America's public schools in the 1940's were: talking, chewing gum, making noise, running in the halls, getting out of turn in line, wearing improper clothing and not putting paper in the waste basket. How things have changed! In the 1990's our school officials are faced with: drug abuse, alcohol abuse, pregnancy, suicide, rape, robbery and assault. Little wonder the streets of our inner cities are stained with the blood of those who uphold the law.

Satan has done his work well in bringing the human race to the precipice of self-destruction. The chief end of this turmoil is to prepare the world for the arrival of the anti-Christ who will bring "Godless order" out of chaos. In all probability he will be an overnight sensation. Be that as it may, believers in Christ must be careful to resist all forms of rebellion against God-given authority. Yes, even in the spiritual things of God, lest we experience the chastening hand of the Lord (I Cor. 11:32; II Cor. 6:9; Heb. 12:6-10).

A DIVINE ILLUSTRATION

"For the husband is the head of the wife, even as Christ is the head of the Church: and He is the Savior of the Body. Therefore, as the Church is subject unto Christ, so let the wives be to their own husbands in every thing" (Eph. 5:23,24).

To illustrate the *authority* that Christ has over the Church the Apostle Paul turns to the marriage relationship. In the beginning God created man from the dust of the earth and breathed into his nostrils the breath of life, and man became a living soul. Shortly after Adam's creation the Lord brought all of the beasts of the field before him that he might name them. This was done for both his and our benefit. Evolutionists, with their unsubstantiated

One Lord

theories, portray early man as an ignoramus making strange grunting sounds. The Bible, however, paints a much different picture. Without the aid of a dictionary or an encyclopedia the first man is said to have given names to every beast of the field. Adam was *brilliant,* and in all likelihood he possessed a greater degree of intelligence than modern man, who has been tainted with the destructive forces of sin.

The first parade of animals also disclosed that there was no suitable companion in the animal kingdom for Adam (Gen. 2:20). Since it is not good for man to be alone God resolved the matter by performing another creative act. After the Lord caused a deep sleep to fall upon Adam He implemented the first surgical procedure by removing a rib from the man's side and creating the woman. If man is refined dust then woman is twice refined! God created her with beauty and grace, which explains why she always wants to look her best in the presence of others. It has been said that the woman was not taken from the sole of the man's foot for she was never to be trampled under foot. Nor was she taken from the skull of her husband due to the fact that she was never to usurp authority over him. The woman was taken from the man's side where she could provide companionship and he could protect her.

To avoid confusion God gave the man and the woman very distinct roles in the marriage relationship. Both are *equally* important but they are vastly different in their scope. By order of creation, the man is given the role of *headship.* Headship involves authority, leadership and most importantly, love. Many have grossly abused this position as an excuse to batter their wives and children.

Hear me and hear me well, God will hold such men accountable for their actions! The role of the husband is to *love* his wife. Leadership that is based upon *love* is leadership she will be more than willing to follow.

The primary responsibility of the home rests upon the shoulders of the man. But, while it is true that the final decision should always be left up to him in important matters, a thoughtful husband will always weigh carefully the counsel of a Godly wife. The Scriptures encourage a husband to live with his wife according to knowledge. He should be well acquainted with those things she fears and her expectations. In other words, a husband should cherish his wife and be sensitive to her every need.

As for the wife's lot, God has given to her the role of *helper,* which calls for submission on her part. Needless to say, this matter is a hot potato in the secular world. Of course, a Godly woman in Christ Jesus understands the importance of obeying the Word of God. Normally the world equates submission with being inferior. This is far from the case, simply because the woman is as capable as the man when it comes to reasoning and making decisions. We must never forget that she too was created in the image of God (Gen. 1:27). Submission is woven throughout the very fabric of our everyday lives. Every time we obey a speed limit sign or pay our taxes we are *submitting* ourselves to the powers that be. Does this make us any less of a person or rob us of our dignity?

For the sake of order, wives are to submit themselves to their *own* husbands. The man completes the woman and likewise the woman the man. She brings to the home refinement—color schemes, curtains and clean windows.

But she is more than a housekeeper; she also is a faithful *companion* who has received numerous gifts from God. Therefore, she should be given the liberty to offer a second opinion on affairs of the household. Pride must never stand in the way of a husband changing his mind if his wife's counsel has merit. If the husband is upholding his responsibility in the home his wife will find security in his leadership. This is important, for the Lord has instilled in the woman the need for stability.

Two women in the same kitchen for any length of time is a recipe for disaster. Why? because there can only be one in charge, otherwise confusion reigns. So it is in the home as well. God does everything decently and in order, thus the head of the woman is the man (I Cor. 11:3). A marriage is built upon trust. Our attitude should never be, this is mine and that is yours; it is better to say, this is *ours*. May love bring us to a oneness of heart, mind and direction.

THE HEADSHIP OF CHRIST

When husbands love their wives they are emulating the Headship of Christ. Love is the controlling factor which governs the authority that Christ has over the Church. In condescending love He left the realms of glory to offer Himself as a once-for-all sacrifice for our sins. As Head of the new creation, Christ is manifesting Himself through the revelation given to Paul. For love's sake, members of the Body of Christ should be willing to *submit* themselves to the Headship of Christ. Is there a woman reading these words who would question Christ's authority over the Church? God forbid! In like manner, the woman should never question her husband's God-given authority, for she is to emulate the Church's submission to Christ. This means that if we desire to walk well-pleasing unto the Lord in the dispensation of Grace, we must *obey* the instructions of Christ found in the Apostle Paul's epistles (I Cor. 14:37). This will ensure spiritual growth as we partake of the riches of God's grace which flow from the pen of Paul. A knowledge of the Word, rightly divided will bring both joy and stability into the Christian experience. And what is God's purpose in all of this?

> "That He might sanctify and cleanse it with the washing of water by the Word. That He might present it to Himself a glorious Church, not having spot, or wrinkle, or any such thing: but that it should be holy and without blemish" (Eph. 5:26,27).

God desires the members of the Body of Christ to live lives separated to Him. As we grow in grace the Word of God will conform us into the image of Christ. Suddenly the things we once deemed so important may now mean absolutely nothing to us. Perhaps it was fancy cars, expensive jewelry or rare collectibles. If we are born again they have been replaced with something infinitely better—CHRIST! On more than one occasion someone has said to this author, "But I just can't remember all of those Scriptures!" My reply is always the same—Keep pouring the water of life into your heart and it will cleanse you from the pollutions of this evil world. What goes in eventually comes out!

Dr. Scofield expressed it beautifully when he wrote, "For the reward of His [Christ's] sacrifice and labor of love He will present the Church to Himself in flawless perfection. . . ." When the trump sounds and the Church which

One Lord

is His Body stands before the Judgment Seat of Christ there will not be a spot or wrinkle or any such flaw. Think of it, no more division among us, for all will be brought into the full light of the preaching of Jesus Christ according to the revelation of the Mystery. The Body will be complete, cleansed of its sin and every saint a "grace believer" in the truest sense of the word!

CHRIST'S AUTHORITY OVER ALL

"Which He wrought in Christ, when He raised Him from the dead, and set Him at His own right hand in the heavenly places, far above all principality, and power, and might, and dominion, and every name that is named, not only in this world, but also in that which is to come" (Eph. 1:20,21).

Another unique feature of the Pauline revelation is that he was the first to reveal what God was doing through Christ at Calvary. Even though the crucifixion was foretold in prophecy, the *significance* of it was kept secret until Paul. Satan himself was totally unaware of what was going to be accomplished at the Cross. When the Devil successfully fueled the hatred of the religious community against Christ they *demanded* His crucifixion. And when the soldiers drove that first nail into the hand of our Savior, Satan was convinced he had finally conquered the Son of God. The fallen host of heaven shouted in triumph—He's dead! He's dead! But to their dismay, three days later He arose from the dead, victorious! *"And having spoiled principalities and powers, he made a shew of them openly, triumphing over them in it"* (Col. 2:15). Talk about a shocking development, these powers of darkness who thought they had defeated Christ became the victims of their own plot. They had sealed their own doom! If they could reverse their evil deed they would be quick to do so, as I Corinthians 2:8 indicates: "Which none of the princes of this world knew [i.e. the hidden wisdom]: for had they known it, they would not have crucified the Lord of glory."

One of the rewards of Christ's resurrection is that He reigns supreme over the powers of the heavens. He is far above all *principalities* who are the supreme rulers of the angelic host. This level of authority would be equivalent to our "joint chiefs of staff." The *powers* are delegated positions and are similar to our higher ranks of officers such as, Colonels, Admirals, Generals, etc. Then we have the realm of *mights* which is the enforcement agency. These are the general troops equal to our four branches of Service—Army, Navy, Air Force and Marines. *Thrones* have to do with seats of authority over various territories, much like a Governor of a state who has the authority to call in the military. Finally, we have *dominions* which are divisions under the thrones and are probably equivalent to our local law enforcement agencies.

One-third of this massive military machine has forsaken its commander in chief—Christ, and has defected to an evil dictator named Satan. Little wonder the apostle warns that "we wrestle not against flesh and blood, but against principalities and powers in the heavenlies." Our enemies are *not* our brothers and sisters in Christ; they are the fallen host of heaven. The only way they can trouble us is when we *allow* sin to have dominion over us. Sometimes believers become Satan's most effective tool! The war has already been won! We are more than con-

One Lord

querors through Jesus Christ our Lord. All we need to do is claim the victory.

There is "one Lord" who can only be fully appreciated through a study of Paul's epistles. It is here we are introduced for the first time to the Headship of Christ over the Church and His position of exaltation in the heavenlies.

11
One Faith

"There is ... One Lord, one faith, one baptism."
—*Ephesians 4:5*

Faith is a divine principle that transcends all dispensational boundaries. In the minds of some, faith is often limited to the expectation of things not yet received. This, indeed, is one of the dimensions of faith, but there is another dimension that the author of Hebrews calls *substance.* "Now faith is the substance of things hoped for, the evidence of things not seen." Substance here simply means that our faith issues from something *tangible.* For example, our belief in eternal life is not based on wishful thinking but rather the living Word of God. Furthermore, we must never lose sight of the testimony of Scripture that God *cannot* lie (Titus 1:2). This is a resounding affirmation that every promise that the Body of Christ possesses will be fully realized at God's appointed time.

Usually we have the tendency to associate *faith* with salvation, and rightfully so. But the Holy Spirit has also reserved another usage which is frequently employed by the Apostle Paul. Here in Eph. 4:5, for instance, the apostle explains how there is only *one faith* in the administration of Grace. Essentially this is a reference to the *doctrines of grace* which were committed solely to Paul to dispense among the Gentiles. Other titles often used in his epistles to emphasize this body of truth are phrases such as, *the faith* and *my gospel.* From this vast new revelation we have chosen to confine our thoughts primarily to our God-given *Commission of Reconciliation.*

THE MINISTRY OF RECONCILIATION

"And all things are of God, who hath reconciled us to Himself by Jesus Christ, and hath given to us the ministry of reconciliation" (II Cor. 5:18).

Reconciliation is a term that is woven throughout the very fabric of our lives. Those of us who have a checking account know the importance of *reconciling* our checkbook balance with the bank statement at the end of each month. Or perhaps two close friends have had a dispute and have not spoken to each other for years. Unexpectedly, they meet one day, begin to talk, and *reconcile* their differences. So then, reconciliation has the idea to change from a state of enmity to friendship or to bring back together.

One of the great Pauline truths that flows from the apostle's pen is, "God was in Christ reconciling the world unto Himself." This implies, of course, that the world was *alienated* from the existence of a holy and righteous God. As we search the Scriptures we learn that there were two stages to this alienation, which made it necessary for mankind to be reconciled with God. The first stage of estrangement takes us back to the very beginning of man's journey through time.

> "Because that, when they knew God, they glorified Him not as God, neither were thankful; but became vain in their imaginations, and their foolish heart was darkened" (Rom. 1:21).

For the first 2500 years of human history God made

Himself known to the Gentile world through Godly men like Abel, Enoch, Methuselah and Noah. So that there would be no question as to His existence due to the absence of any written revelation, God also made His will known by signs and wonders in the heavens above (Ps. 19:1-4). The Gentiles' response to the things of God was anything but favorable. Their disdain for the Holy One of heaven culminated in the construction of the Tower of Babel, which stands forever as a monument to the evil of mankind. Paul says concerning those days, ". . . that when they KNEW God [i.e. about Him], they glorified Him not as God."

Could it be that man was so primitive that he could not comprehend what was being imparted to him? A brief study of ancient civilizations will dismiss this argument in short order. Take the pyramids that were constructed along the Nile, the likes of which still baffle the intellectuals of our day. They demonstrate that the Egyptians had extraordinary knowledge of both geometry and astronomy. We are told that these tombs of the kings were built with such precision that the temperature in the center of each tomb remains a constant 60 degrees, even in the heat of mid-afternoon.

"Professing themselves to be wise, they became fools" and turned their backs in unbelief. Thus, God withdrew His blessing, leaving the world in a state of alienation. Three pronouncements were made upon the Gentiles in Rom. 1:24,26,28 which resulted in a hopeless condition:

> "Wherefore God ALSO gave them up to uncleanness through the lust of their own hearts. . . .

> "For this cause God gave them up unto vile affections. . . .

One Faith

"God gave them over to a reprobate mind, to do those things which are not convenient."

The second stage of alienation came with God's chosen nation Israel. Out of the ashes of Babel God raised up Abraham, who became the father of a new nation. Then for 1500 years God made Himself known through the prophets who recorded His will in the pages of the Old Testament canon. *"What advantage then hath the Jew?"* Paul says, "Much in every way: chiefly, because that unto them were committed the oracles of God."

The hope of the world was invested in Israel, but pride hindered her from being the light to the world that God had intended her to be. The outcome was catastrophic, for she went about seeking to establish her own righteousness apart from God. The chosen nation blatantly ignored the prophets, rejected her Messiah and murdered Stephen, who was calling for her repentance. Yes, she too rebelled against God and turned her back on His righteousness. Therefore, God tossed her aside in unbelief like a piece of broken furniture (Rom. 11:7-12,15,30).

Rest assured that there will never be a greater crisis past, present or future, than that hour when the *whole world* found itself alienated from God. Mankind was wandering aimlessly in darkness, unaware that the next step was the eternal wrath of God in the Lake of Fire. But God has done a wonderful thing on the world's behalf. He has provided a detour that we will call the *road of reconciliation*. As the world travels down this road there are exits both to the right and to the left. The exit to the left leads to everlasting condemnation, while the exit on the right leads to Christ and eternal life. The road of reconciliation cannot save anyone; however, it does lead the sinner to the pathway of salvation which is in Christ Jesus.

For those who are slipping away to a Christless eternity, there may be only a few opportunities left to trust Christ before the end of the road! "Believe on the Lord Jesus Christ and thou shalt be saved."

IMPUTATION

> "To wit, that God was in Christ, reconciling the world unto Himself, not imputing their trespasses unto them. . ." (II Cor. 5:19).

God then has directed all His enemies down the road of reconciliation, that they *all* might have an opportunity to be saved from their sins. He has even removed a barrier to assist them on their journey. During the present dispensation of Grace, God is *not* imputing the trespasses of His enemies to them. This is a blessing in disguise, since sin is so commonplace today. If the above were not the case, most would be in danger of the swift retribution of God before having much exposure to the gospel.

From time to time under the Law God *did* impute the sins of His adversaries as a solemn warning of His displeasure. When the children of Israel committed the sin of *idolatry* and worshipped the golden calf, three thousand fell at the edge of the sword (Ex. 32:27,28). Miriam was stricken with leprosy right before the eyes of her brother Aaron for *murmuring* against Moses (Num. 12:1-10). Then there was Nadab and Abihu, who offered strange fire upon the altar of God and were consumed by fire themselves for *disobeying* the Word of the Lord (Lev. 10:1-3). The sin of Achan who kept back the wedge of gold ended up in his death by stoning (Josh. 7:25,26).

We should add that God's offer of reconciliation includes a *revocable* clause concerning the sins of His enemies. That is to say, if the unbeliever rejects His generous offer of reconciliation and subsequent salvation, then their sins are kept in store until the day of judgment. In that day God will render to every man according to his deeds (Rom. 2:5,6).

As we have seen, alienation is two-way, in that man turned his back on God followed by God withdrawing His blessing, first from the Gentiles, then from the nation Israel. In like manner, reconciliation is two-way but in reverse. God graciously took the initiative to provide a thoroughfare of reconciliation, but the sinner must exercise his human responsibility to make the reconciliation *complete*. This is accomplished by trusting Christ, who is the *way*, the truth and the life. In this way, reconciliation does indeed merge into salvation.

AMBASSADORS FOR CHRIST

"Now then we are ambassadors for Christ, as though God did beseech you by us: we pray you in Christ's stead, be ye reconciled to God" (II Cor. 5:20).

Such a glorious message as reconciliation must at all cost be taken with haste to the unsaved masses. This is precisely what God did when He *commissioned* us as *ambassadors* for Christ. I read some time ago that in the Roman empire there were two types of provinces—senatorial and imperial. The senatorial provinces were peaceful for the most part, and never caused Rome any problem. This could not be said of the imperial ones, for they were dangerous and frequently rebelled against the empire. It was to the imperial provinces that Rome sent ambassadors to help ease tension and announce the emperor's objectives. They were some of the first diplomats in the truest sense of the term.

In the present evil age in which we live the world is an imperial province that has nothing but contempt for God. In the midst of this tumult God has sent in His ambassadors to offer the world's weary warriors of rebellion *amnesty*.

What an honor it would be to be chosen by the President of the United States to serve our country as an ambassador in a foreign land. Every ambassador seems to have three outstanding characteristics. First, they always look *presentable*. Secondly, they are *dignified*. And finally, they are *well informed* as to the goals of the commander in chief. If this is true in the affairs of men, how much more so as we represent Christ in His absence. Many in the world are dull of hearing and therefore need to hear again that God loves them and has reconciled them unto Himself. Unlike the Great Commission given to Israel, our commission does not concern nations but individuals within the nations. Begin by committing the word of reconciliation to your loved ones and remember that the mission field extends into foreign lands as well.

What has happened to the missionary zeal that was cradled in our country? The fires have seemingly gone out except for a few flickering embers that yet glow. Pray that God will ignite a fire in our hearts for lost souls in other lands. Permit me to say that far too often our Grace Missionaries struggle on meager salaries that would probably be below the poverty level in this country. They have left family and friends and the security of our homeland to

One Faith

preach Christ to those who are less fortunate than ourselves. The very least we can do is to *encourage* them with our *financial* support and *pray* without ceasing for their needs.

I suppose the polar caps will melt before the denominational churches of North America would come to their assistance, for reasons that are obvious. We must rise to the occasion on their behalf before the doors of third-world countries are completely closed. Even as I write some mission boards are recalling their missionaries in certain countries, due to Muslim threats of death to those who proclaim the good news of Jesus Christ.

A herculean task lies before us to spread the *word of reconciliation*. And may it ever be before us that ". . . if one died for all, then were all dead." Can it be truthfully said that *all* who have been born of the woman are born in sin and therefore spiritually dead? Then as the apostle says, Christ died for all *without exception* (II Cor. 5:14,15). Yes, Christ died for *you!* "Now is the accepted time, **NOW IS THE DAY OF SALVATION.**" How many would you say have died in the last 24 hours around the world? Tomorrow death may tap you on the shoulder and say, "Your hour has come." Time is of the essence; to receive God's wonderful offer of reconciliation, simply believe that Christ died for *your* sins *personally* and rose again the third day for *your* justification. Do it today, eternity awaits.

12
One Baptism

"There is . . . One Lord, one faith, one baptism."
—Ephesians 4:5

Those who minister full time in the Lord's work seldom hesitate to acknowledge that *confusion reigns supreme* when it comes to the subject of *water baptism*. This becomes very evident when we consider the multiplicity of views held by the denominations on the matter. For example, *Catholicism* believes that baptism washes away original sin. *Lutherans* would take issue with this, for they teach that it makes the recipient a child of the covenant. The *Church of Christ* holds that water baptism is a requirement for salvation. "Hold on," says the *Baptist*, "Salvation is by grace through faith; baptism is merely an outward sign of an inward work of grace."

The confusion deepens when the discussion turns to whether or not infants should be baptized. *Presbyterians* and the *Reformed* are emphatic that they should be, while the *Baptists* and the *Bible Churches of America,* generally speaking, denounce such a practice, claiming that only believing adults should be permitted to observe this ceremony. Furthermore, it is all-out war when the topic shifts to *how* the water should be applied. The *Reformed* defend the mode of sprinkling to which the *Baptists* and the *Independents* object because they believe they can substantiate immersion from the Scriptures. Many of the

Methodists disagree on both counts, on the basis that in the Old Testament they poured the oil and the blood, therefore, pouring is the proper method.

The *Baptists,* who are perhaps the leading champions of the water rite, cannot even agree among themselves. This became evident to me some years ago when I served as a *Baptist* deacon. One of our families, who was in good standing in the assembly, had moved away and naturally in the course of time wanted to join the local *Baptist* church in their area. However, to their dismay they were *refused membership.* The new assembly *required* that they be placed under the water *three times:* once in the name of the Father, once in the name of the Son, and once in the name of the Holy Spirit.

We do not doubt that all of these groups are sincere in their convictions and well-meaning in their use of the Word of God to confirm their positions. But something is surely amiss, for we know that God is *not* the author of confusion, yet confusion does indeed reign (I Cor. 14:33). Has the Church overlooked something in its search for the truth? Sad to say, it has lost track of the *key* that unlocks the sacred secret—namely Paul's gospel. The question is not whether or not water baptism is taught in the Word of God; *all* agree it is. The real question is, should it be *practiced at all* in the dispensation of Grace? Is it possible that God *never* intended water baptism to be observed during this dispensation? This certainly would explain why there is so much confusion over the matter.

To discover the mind and will of God on similar issues the *Bereans* searched the Scriptures daily, studying to see if these things were so. Following their example let's turn to Hebrews 9:10.

THE PURPOSE OF WATER BAPTISM

"Which stood only in meats and drinks, and divers washings, and carnal ordinances, imposed on them until the time of reformation" (Heb. 9:10).

To begin with we want to establish the purpose of water baptism when it was in operation. The theme of the ninth chapter of Hebrews is how the Old Testament types were merely shadows of the reality that we now enjoy in Christ. The Apostle Paul instructs us how the Law contained numerous ordinances which were a means of worshipping God (Heb. 9:1). One of those ordinances imposed upon the people of God under the Law was called *"divers washings."* If you consult one of your Greek word studies you will find that the word *washings* in the original language is *BAPTISMOS*. Subsequently, the Holy Spirit reveals through the pen of Paul that water baptism was one of the "ordinances of divine service." This also indicates that the ritual of baptism did *not* begin with John the Baptist, contrary to popular belief.

Having established the above, we now want to proceed to the Old Testament where the Lord initiates one of the first *water ceremonies.*

"And this is the thing thou shalt do unto them to hallow them, to minister unto me in the priest's office. . . . And Aaron and his sons thou shalt bring unto the door of the tabernacle of the congregation, and shalt wash them with water" (Ex. 29:1,4).

God ordained under the Law that the Levites were to be inducted into the priesthood by being brought to the door of the tabernacle and washed, or *baptized,* publicly before the entire congregation. After all, they were going to be ministering in the holy things of God, therefore, it was essential that they be *consecrated* publicly to their office. For the rest of the story, however, we must turn to Exodus 19:6 where Israel as a nation was promised to be a *kingdom of priests.*

> "And ye shall be unto me a kingdom of priests, and an holy nation. These are the words which thou shalt speak unto the children of Israel" (Ex. 19:6).

Walking down the corridor of time from the life of Moses to the days of John the Baptist, John called Israel to repentance that she might be prepared to become that *kingdom of priests* referred to 1,500 years earlier. But first, these believing Israelites had to be baptized with water to induct them into the priesthood. This explains why *all* of Judea went out to be baptized of John. Since baptism was *required* by God to express their faith, those declining to be washed are said to have *rejected* the counsel of God against themselves, thus they perished in their sins (Mark 16:16; Luke 7:28-30). In that *future* millennial kingdom all Israelites will be priests ministering in the things of God—that is their confident expectation.

Permit me to ask: Are you looking to be one of the priests of God in the establishment of the thousand-year kingdom on the earth? As a Gentile writing primarily to Gentiles, during God's parenthetical period of Grace, *our hope* is to be with Christ in the heavenlies, which will be fully realized at the *Rapture.* Since we are members of the Body of Christ, the commandment to be baptized in order to become a kingdom of priests is *not* binding upon us today. We are a new creation in Christ Jesus with a heavenly hope.

The second reason John came baptizing with water was that Christ might take center stage in the affairs of men.

> "And I knew Him not: but that He should be made manifest to Israel, therefore am I come baptizing with water" (John 1:31).

Every time John *sprinkled* repentant Israelites with water he declared to them that the Messiah, spoken of by the prophets of old, had come and was in their midst (Ezek. 36:25; Isa. 52:15). John was the forerunner of Christ, preparing the way before Him that all of the house of Israel might know assuredly that Jesus was the Christ, the Son of God.

Surely this feature of water baptism cannot be followed on the simple premise that Israel as a nation has been *set aside in unbelief* and that her King is presently rejected and is a Royal exile (Rom. 11:7,20,26-32; I Pet. 2:7,8; Eph. 1:20,21).

Finally, John baptized in the river Jordan to *symbolically* cleanse Israel of her sins.

> "John did baptize in the wilderness, and preach the baptism of repentance for the remission of sins . . . . and [they] were all baptized of him in the river of Jordan, confessing their sins" (Mark 1:4,5).

Their submission to the rite of baptism demonstrated that they were sinners who were guilty of breaking their *covenant relationship* with Almighty God. They came in droves to have their sins washed away, desiring to be right with God. Under grace the shadow has now given way to the reality of the finished work of Christ. Through Paul's revelation we understand that we have the forgiveness of our sins through the shed blood of Christ (Rom. 3:25; Eph. 1:7). Consequently, all the oceans of water in the world could never wash away one sin. To teach that water baptism today symbolically cleanses from sin is to *minimize* the meritorious work of Christ at Calvary.

Every believer needs to humbly accept that it is *impossible* to observe these commandments during the dispensation of Grace. May we most reverently submit ourselves to this blessed truth.

A NEW ADMINISTRATION

"For Christ sent me not to baptize, but to preach the gospel: not with wisdom of words, lest the cross of Christ should be made of none effect" (I Cor. 1:17).

The child of God will never grasp that water baptism is not for today until he first comes to see that God has instituted a new program for the Body of Christ. As we have seen, this program is known as the *Mystery*. Through *progressive revelations* it was disclosed to the Apostle Paul that the ordinance of water baptism was to be *superseded* by the finished work of Christ.

Little wonder Paul declares: *"I thank God I baptized none of you, but Crispus and Gaius. . . . For Christ sent me not to baptize,"* but to preach the good news of Christ and Him crucified (I Cor. 1:14-17). Neither Peter, James, John, nor any others of those under the kingdom program, for that matter, could have said that they were "not sent to baptize." According to their program, that would have been the same as saying, "I thank God that none of you are saved." For as the Scriptures themselves set forth under the old economy baptism was a requirement for their salvation. Please note carefully the Holy Spirit's order in Mark 16:16, *"He that believeth* [Jesus is the Son of God—John 20:31] *and is baptized* [for the remission of their sins—Mk. 1:4,5] *shall* [then] *be saved; but he that believeth not shall be damned."*

God does not want us to place our faith in dead works, which never had the power to save to begin with. Instead, He wants us to *trust* in Christ, who is the new and living way. Paul's gospel draws back the veil from our understanding so that we can begin to appreciate the riches of God's grace, how that God was in Christ reconciling the world unto Himself. As the hymn writer appropriately says, "Calvary covers it all."

But some will inquire, "Isn't water baptism an outward sign of an inward happening?" I used to say that as well until my eyes were opened to the fact that such a teaching is found *nowhere* in the Scriptures. Could it be that many *unsuspecting* saints have been following the teachings and commandments of men? Tradition oftentimes binds men hand and foot to a religious system which hinders them from coming to the *truth*.

We've been told, "But Paul was baptized and he baptized others—so there!" Paul also circumcised; would we be in the will of God if we practiced religious circumcision today? Certainly not! Once it was understood that this ordinance was fulfilled in Christ it was discontinued, which is a generally-accepted fact (Col. 2:11). Paul also took a Jewish vow. Who among us has not taught that this has also passed away with the advent of grace? (Col.

2:14). Paul performed miraculous demonstrations, signs and wonders as well. But who can deny these too faded away with the advance of the present dispensation? (I Cor. 13:10; Col. 1:25).

Why is it that the Church is more than willing, for the most part, to acknowledge that circumcision, Jewish vows and demonstrative miracles have passed with the old economy, but still *clings* to water baptism? The answer is really quite simple: It is in the nature of man to want to *do* something. May we ever be mindful of the blessed truth that *grace* is the essence of salvation *without doing anything* (Rom. 4:5; Eph. 2:8,9; Titus 3:5).

> "Blotting out the handwriting of ordinances that was against us, which was contrary to us, and took it out of the way, nailing it to His cross" (Col. 2:14).

Most will agree that water baptism is an *ordinance,* this is rarely disputed. If this be so, and we believe it is, then what Christ accomplished at Calvary *blotted out* or removed the ritual of water baptism. Which would you prefer if you were near starvation, a beautiful picture of a sumptuous dinner or the *real* thing? Thanks be unto God we are feasting on the riches of His grace.

IDENTIFICATION

> "Know ye not, that so many of us as were baptized into Jesus Christ were baptized into His death? Therefore we are buried with Him by baptism into death: that like as Christ was raised up from the dead by the glory of the Father, even so we also should walk in newness of life" (Rom. 6:3,4).

The doctrine of *identification* is another unique feature of the Pauline revelation. We are taught here in Romans that we have been "baptized into Jesus Christ." This, of course, is our *spiritual baptism* into Christ and therefore is the *one baptism* spoken of in Ephesians 4:5. The purpose of this baptism is twofold:

1. It places us into the Body of Christ where we become *one* with Him. Hence, we are joined to an organism which has a common source of life, and that life is Christ. Since we are *identified* with Christ in this manner *all* believers have been baptized by the same Spirit. *All* share the same inheritance. *All* have been made to drink of the same Spirit and *all* share the same hope, which is Christ (Gal. 2:20; I Cor. 12:13,27).

2. We are also *identified* with Christ's death, burial and resurrection. When our Savior was hanging on the Cross our old man was crucified with Him. His death was our death. Thus, God performed a spiritual circumcision at the Cross, which is precisely what the apostle says, "In whom also ye are circumcised with the circumcision made without hands, in putting off the body of the sins of the flesh by the circumcision of Christ" (Col. 2:11). Circumcision means to cut away. So, when Christ was cut off at Calvary the body of our sins or the old man was cut off as well.

As far as God is concerned the old man has been buried with Christ in Joseph's tomb never to be heard of again. And that glorious morning when Christ rose from the dead our *new man* is said to have risen with Him. This *spiritual baptism* is an operation of God and has absolutely nothing to do with a water ceremony (Col. 2:12,13). We are *complete in Christ* to the praise of His glory!

Inasmuch as this is a positional truth then, we have the right, and a responsibility to take God at His Word. Hence, we are to *occupy* that position and appropriate the blessings accordingly. Having understood what we enjoy in Christ positionally should translate into a desire to live a godly life. We are to reckon ourselves "dead indeed to sin, but alive unto God. . . ."

AMAZING GRACE!

"Amazing grace! how sweet the sound
   That saved a wretch like me!
I once was lost, but now am found,
   Was blind, but now I see.

" 'Twas grace that taught my heart to fear,
   And grace my fears relieved;
How precious did that grace appear
   The hour I first believed!

"Through many dangers, toils and snares,
   I have already come;
'Tis grace hath brought me safe thus far,
   And grace will lead me home."

—John Newton

13
One God

> "There is . . . One God and Father of all, who is above all, and through all, and in you all."
> —*Ephesians 4:6*

The seventh unity of the Spirit confirms that the Apostle Paul believed that there is only *one God*. Many, of course, have difficulty reconciling this with the fact that God is also a Trinity. Someone once said concerning the Trinity: "If you try to explain it you will lose your mind; if you deny it you will lose your soul." There are many things in this life that I fail to fully understand, but that doesn't mean they are not so. I marvel every time I pick up the telephone receiver and talk to someone across the country. It is nothing short of phenomenal how the sound of my voice can travel so many miles through a wire. But who can deny that this is indeed a wonder of modern technology.

The Bible emphatically teaches us that there is one God who eternally exists in three persons: Father, Son and Holy Spirit. Even though this goes far beyond our comprehension we nevertheless accept it by faith, because this is the plain teaching of the Word of God. It is helpful to remember that God has stamped His creation with countless trinities, each of which bear testimony that the concept of the Trinity does not go beyond reason. Scientists, for example, inform us that the universe is made up of basically three components: space, time and matter. But how many universes do we have—ONE! Water can be transformed into a solid (ice), a vapor or into a liquid. Three forms but still water! When God created man in the beginning He created him a trinity—body, soul and spirit. One of the facets then of being created in the image of God is that we too are a trichotomy.

THE FATHERHOOD OF GOD

"One God and Father of all..." (Eph. 4:6).

There are some who incorrectly assume that God is the Father of the whole human race. A case in point are those in the religious community who frequently use the phrase, "The Fatherhood of God and the brotherhood of man." Needless to say, this teaching is a subtle attack upon the truth. Nowhere in the Scriptures is God referred to as the heavenly Father of the unbeliever. As a matter of fact, the words of our Lord to the unbelieving religious leaders of His day are worthy of our attention here:

> "Jesus said unto them, If God were your Father, ye would love me: for I proceeded forth and came from God; neither came I of myself, but He sent me. Why do ye not understand my speech? even because ye cannot hear my word. Ye are of your father the devil, and the lusts of your father ye will do. He was a murderer from the beginning, and abode not in the truth, because there is no truth in him. When he speaketh a lie, he speaketh of his own: for he is a liar, and the father of it" (John 8:42-44).

This stinging rebuke indicates that these ungodly leaders refused to receive the Lord. Consequently, they were intolerant of the notion that they were of *their father* the devil. The Master went on to add, "He that is of God heareth God's words: ye therefore hear them not, because ye are not of God." Contrary to popular belief, God is not the Father of those who spurn His love and cast doubt upon the counsel of His will. Unbelievers do have a father, but he is said to be the devil! And rightfully so, for they have followed Satan in his rebellion against God. The Apostle Paul concurs, stating that those who are dead in trespasses and sins ". . . walk according to the course of this world, according to the prince of the power of the air, the spirit that now worketh in the children of disobedience" (Eph. 2:2).

Bringing our thoughts back to Ephesians 4:6, when the apostle makes a reference to God being the *Father of all,* dispensationally he has a specific group in mind. The revelation that there is only *one God* and Father is a well established fact throughout Holy Scripture. What is often overlooked, however, is that a further revelation was given to Paul, in that God had *predetermined* before the foundation of the world to bring into existence a new entity known as the Body of Christ (Eph. 1:4,5). This has now been manifest through Paul's gospel where we also learn the members of His Body have received a *heavenly inheritance.* Yes, God is the Father of believing Israel. However, the *all* of Ephesians 4:6 is to be *limited* to the believers of this age in which we are living.

When a father is handed his newborn son a new relationship is created that can never be broken. Whether in life or death the lad will always be the son of his father. Similarly, upon regeneration we are born from above into the family of God. So, it can be appropriately said that

God is our Father and we have become His sons. Normally a father is a role model who provides for the future of his children. The same is true in the spiritual realm; we are heirs of God and joint heirs with Christ, which springs from our relationship with the Father.

A PAULINE VIEW OF GOD

> ". . . Who is above all, and through all, and in you all" (Eph. 4:6).

The *transcendence* and *immanence* of God are rich theological terms that describe two precious truths concerning our heavenly Father. The transcendence of God simply means that God transcends or is far *above* and *beyond* His creation. He is sovereign, eternal, being infinite in holiness, righteousness, wisdom and knowledge. God's *supremacy* is clearly seen in Daniel 4:35 where the prophet states:

> "And all the inhabitants of the earth are reputed as nothing: and He doeth according to His will in the army of heaven, and among the inhabitants of the earth: and none can stay His hand, or say unto Him, What doest Thou?"

Peering into the heavens through a powerful telescope only serves to show how insignificant man is in relation to the universe around him. Astronomers could only shake their heads in amazement when they discovered that there are other galaxies beyond the Milky Way. To whom shall we attribute the wonders of the starry heavens? And who placed the earth the precise distance from the sun? None other than the Lord God Almighty! Personally, we take great comfort in the sovereignty of God, that He is in control of all things.

The immanence of God teaches us that God is *actively* involved in the lives of His own. Paul makes this explicitly clear in the above passage when he says that God is working "through all," that is, *through* each member of the Body of Christ. Obviously the Apostle Paul did not hold to a *deistic* view of God. Deism denies that God exercises a constant providential control over His creation and that He never answers the prayers of His children.[1]

The epistles of St. Paul abound with references as to how God is actively involved in both the spiritual and physical aspects of our lives. God is well pleased when He acts in response to our prayers, as it is according to His will, of course. Being blessed with all spiritual blessings does not negate His willingness to supply for our physical needs as well.

When I assumed the responsibility of my first pastorate, the church to which I was called was struggling to make ends meet. To avoid being a burden to the assembly my wife and I agreed to only accept a very modest salary. For the most part we fared pretty well but there were times that we were scraping the bottom of the barrel. Due to a number of unexpected expenses there was one particular month when we were considerably short of meeting our budget. Sometimes the Lord allows these times to come our way to cause us to rely more fully upon Him. Thus, we took the matter before the throne of Grace, beseeching our Father above to intervene on our behalf. The only ones who knew about our plight was God and us! One week to the day a check arrived in the mail for the exact amount needed from an acquaintance of my father

---

1. Lectures in Systematic Theology, Thiessen. Pages 74, 75.

whom we did not even know. They simply felt lead of the Lord to send us a gift! Little did they know that they were an answer to prayer! Yes, God takes delight in caring for all of His children.

Who could fail to see that God also *intervened* in the case of Epaphroditus. ".. *He was sick nigh unto death: but God had mercy on him...*" (Phil. 2:27). It is strongly implied that the Philippians, and Paul himself, prayed for this dear brother that God would raise him up, and indeed he did—in connection with their prayers. And note: God healed Epaphroditus for Paul's sake too, "... lest I should have sorrow upon sorrow." It should be added here that the recovery of Epaphroditus was not due to the natural healing process that is programmed into the body. Rather it was a direct result of GOD'S MERCY upon him and Paul. Had God not *intervened* Ephaphroditus undoubtedly would have died.

We should be careful to add that many times the response we receive back from heaven in answer to our prayers is "My grace is sufficient for thee...." In this event we are able to take comfort in the truth that, "... the peace of God, which passeth all understanding, shall keep your hearts and minds through Christ Jesus."

We are to understand that sometimes God has a *higher purpose* in mind for not healing our loved one or Christian friend. It is not necessarily a lack of faith on the petitioner's part. Possibly, the affliction is allowed as a test or perhaps to draw the individual into a closer walk with the Lord. Sometimes it's to bring a family closer together or even more importantly that God's strength might be made perfect in our weakness. Whatever the case may be, may

God receive all the honor and glory that is due His name (II Cor. 12:7-10).

Shall we bind the hands of God today to say that He will never heal the sick or supply our needs in answer to our prayers? Paul's revelation and experience unite to declare otherwise. Our heavenly Father is a loving Father who wants us to bring all of our cares before Him. Such is the case with any father. He is interested in every detail of our lives, including those seemingly incidental things.

THE TEMPLE OF GOD

Another precious gem that we unearth from Paul's revelation is the fascinating truth that every member of the Body of Christ is indwelt by the Godhead.

"One God and Father . . . who . . . [dwelleth] in you all" (Eph. 4:6).

". . . Christ in you, the hope of glory" (Col. 1:27).

"What? know ye not that your body is the temple of the Holy Ghost which is in you. . ." (I Cor. 6:19).

The foregoing passages were undoubtedly the inspiration behind Alfred Ackley's famous hymn "He Lives." Most of us know the chorus by heart:

"He lives, He lives, Christ Jesus lives today!

"He walks with me and talks with me along life's narrow way.

"He lives, He lives, salvation to impart!

"You ask me how I know He lives? He lives within my heart."

It is a solemn thought that this temple we call the body

One God

is the very place that God resides. In the Old Testament the temple was the depository for the Oracles of God, whereas under grace the Word of God is available to all who desire to store it in their hearts by faith. Furthermore, the temple was a holy place where daily sacrifices were offered, which should prompt us to ". . . present our bodies a living sacrifice, holy, acceptable unto God. . . ."

Every place we go, every thought we think, and every word we speak, is done in the presence of God. This should give us the highest motivation to live a Godly life that is well pleasing unto the Lord. What we do with our lives *now* will have far reaching affects at the Judgment Seat of Christ. The author has been asked on more than one occasion as to why God does not judge the believer when he dies. Why wait until the day of Christ? The answer is really quite simple—our works and influence follow us long after our demise.

Pastor J. C. O'Hair is a classic example that even though he is dead, he yet speaketh! Brother O'Hair wrote numerous booklets that are still reaching the confused masses with the revelation of the Mystery, not to mention the saints who are being edified by his Bible lessons on tape. As we can see, the final chapter in the life of Pastor O'Hair's accomplishments is yet being written. The same is also true of those who die in unbelief. Al Capone is well known here in Chicago as the godfather of organized crime. Though he passed away in 1947, the infamous underworld he created is still corrupting the lives of men and women to this very day. Thus, the book recording the evil deeds of Al Capone is yet incomplete.

When time slips into eternity God has "... appointed a day, in which he will judge the world in righteousness...." Therefore, one is prudent to trust Christ early in life and surrender completely to the Lord's will. In what way will you, dear reader, meet your Maker? Will you step into His presence and know Him as your Father or will you tremble at the sight of Him as He prepares to execute wrath upon His enemies? The final outcome rests with you. Believe on the Lord Jesus Christ!

14
Our Blessed Hope

"Looking for that blessed hope, and the glorious appearing of the great God and our Savior Jesus Christ."
—*Titus 2:13*

In the springtime of our lives we often fail to spend enough time meditating upon the wonderful truth of the Rapture. But as the winds of change reshape the seasons of life we quickly become more mindful of this promise. This is especially true when we begin to lose loved ones and Christian friends—as one by one they leave this old world behind. Thus, we eagerly await Christ's return in the Rapture, not merely to be delivered from the presence of sin, although this we anticipate, but to be "with Christ, which is far better."

As I pen these words my family is sound asleep with the hands of Father Time approaching one o'clock in the morning. Such occasions have a way of giving rise to the thought—perhaps tonight the Lord will come for His Church. As I sit here I wonder if heaven is astir in preparation for the glorious event. The late hour has not brought me to the point of delirium; I'm just meditating a moment upon the motto above my study door, "Perhaps today!" Though the time of Christ's arrival is unknown, the order of events that will transpire in that day are well documented. Since this documentation, for the most part, is found in I Thessalonians we shall confine our thoughts to what Paul wrote to those at Thessalonica.

WORDS OF COMFORT

"But I would not have you to be ignorant, brethren, concerning them which are asleep, that ye sorrow not, even as others which have no hope" (I Thes. 4:13).

Paul's apostolic journeys led him to numerous cities, one of which was Thessalonica in the province of Macedonia. As was his custom after leading his hearers to a saving knowledge of Christ, without delay he delivered unto them the *Blessed Hope*. This was the better part of wisdom, for the apostle knew that after his departure the saints would be called upon to suffer for the cause of Christ. As long as these new converts had hope they could endure all things. In the case of those at Thessalonica, some of their loved ones were unexpectedly visited by death, which naturally raised the question—what hope, if any, will they have?

Paul comforted them that they should "sorrow not even as others which have no hope." It is natural to mourn the passing of a loved one, but we do not sorrow as the unbeliever to the point of *despair*.

"For if we believe that Jesus died and rose again, even so them also which sleep in Jesus will God bring with Him."

There is indeed life beyond the grave, according to this passage. When death claims a child of God his *soul* and *spirit* survive the demise of the body. Thus, to be absent from the body is to be present with the Lord (II Cor. 5:8). Furthermore, whenever we visit a funeral home to pay our last respects to a friend who is lying in state, he has the appearance of being *asleep.* Paul's usage then of the term *sleep* is a reference to the body, not to the soul, which ascends back to God who gave it. This is further substantiated by the fact that the dead in Christ are said to return with Him in the Rapture (I Thes. 4:16). Based on the terms of salvation given in verse 14, (which by the way are exclusively Pauline), we are to conclude that only the Body of Christ will be partakers of this momentous event.

THE SECRET COMING OF CHRIST

"For the Lord Himself shall descend from heaven with a shout, with the voice of the archangel, and with the trump of God: and the dead in Christ shall rise first" (I Thes. 4:16).

Perhaps we should begin by calling attention to a serious error that is frequently made by many dispensationalists. A great deal of confusion has been generated down through the years by those who make the pretribulational Rapture synonymous with the Second Coming of Christ to the earth. Let us settle here once and for all that the Rapture and the Second Coming of Christ are *not* one and the same, nor should it be said that the Rapture is the first phase of the Second Advent.

The *upward calling* of the Church, which is His Body, and the Second Coming are separated by a period of seven years called the tribulation. Therefore, what God has *separated* let no man join together. Because this blunder is so prevalent, this writer has adopted the phrase "the Secret Coming of Christ" to help the reader distinguish between these two events. It is a *secret or unprophesied event* in the sense that the world will not behold the *invis-*

ible return of the Savior. Nor is there any indication that the graves of the dead in Christ will be left open as in the first resurrection preceding the millennium (John 5:28,29 cf. Matt. 27:51-53). This four thousand year old secret was hidden in the mind of God until made known through the ministry of St. Paul. Thus, the pretribulational Rapture is also to be added to the collection of the unsearchable riches of Christ.

1. THE TRUMP OF GOD

As mentioned in the foregoing lines, one of the main features of the Secret Coming is that it will be invisible to the inhabitants of the earth. Since the Lord will remain in the upper atmosphere, we are *caught off* of the earth into heaven (I Thes. 4:17). The sequence of events will begin with the sounding of the trump. In the Old Testament the trumpets were used accordingly: First, they were blown to gather the congregation of Israel to the door of the tabernacle to meet with the Lord. Secondly, when an enemy approached they were sounded to warn the camp to prepare for battle. Thirdly, the trumpets were blown in the days of Israel's gladness, such as when Solomon's temple was completed in Jerusalem (Num. 10:1-10; II Chron. 5:12-14).

By way of application, when the trump of God is sounded at the Rapture it will result in our gathering together unto the Lord. Also, in all probability this blast of the trump will be heard by the world as God *breaks* the silence of this dispensation to declare war on His enemies. The significance of this chilling sound will be understood all too soon as God prepares to pour out His wrath on this Christ-rejecting world (Ps. 2:1-5). Lastly, the Rapture will

Our Blessed Hope

be our day of gladness as we step into the very presence of the Lord, who loved us and gave Himself for us. As the hymn writer has expressed it, "What a day of rejoicing that will be!"

2. THE SECRET RESURRECTION

Simultaneously with the sounding of the trump the Lord will descend with a shout, at which time the dead in Christ will be brought forth. We have the highest admiration for Dr. Scofield, who has taken great strides in furthering our understanding of dispensational truth. It must be remembered, however, that he was *not* fully aware of Paul's gospel, which is clearly evidenced by his comments on the passages under consideration. "Not church saints only, but all bodies of the saved, of whatever dispensation, are included in the first resurrection...as described here...."[1]

The *secret* resurrection that will take place at the Rapture should never be confused with the *first* resurrection at the Second Coming of Christ. Those who rightly divide the Word of truth now see that only the members of the Body of Christ will be raised at the Rapture. The terms of salvation outlined in I Thessalonians 4:14 and the phrase, "dead in Christ" (i.e. the deceased members of the Body of Christ), limits this prestigious group to the Church of this age. To avoid raising all of the prophetic saints including the unsaved, our Lord apparently will specify the Body of Christ by name. A good example of this is when the Master raised Lazarus: He purposely called him by name, lest all of the dead march forth from the grave.

---

1. The *Old Scofield Reference Bible,* page 1269.

So then, all of the members of Christ's Body, from Paul to the present, will be raised first and given their glorified bodies. Then we who ". . . are alive and remain shall be *caught up* together with them in the clouds. . . ." There is going to be one generation (perhaps ours!) which shall escape the clutches of death and be changed in a moment of the twinkling of an eye.

3. CAUGHT UP TOGETHER

> "Behold, I show you a mystery; We shall not all sleep, but we shall all be changed, In a moment, in the twinkling of an eye. . ." (I Cor. 15:51,52).

Here Paul describes that it will only take "a moment" to gloriously transform these bodies of humiliation. Interestingly, the Greek construction of this phrase is EN ATOMOS, a scientific term for an atom which was considered indivisible. Simultaneously, we will be transported to glory in the "twinkling of an eye," which E. W. Vine defines as "any rapid movement." So, it might be correctly said that we will be changed in *a moment,* which is so sudden that it is an increment of time that is indivisible! Moreover, the speed of our translation to heaven from earth cannot even be measured, only to say that it will be *instantaneous.*

Turning a moment to the phrase "caught up," we find that there are various shades of meaning of this expression in the so-called New Testament and each of them can be applied in one way or another to the Rapture.[2] The Spirit of the Lord is said to have "caught away Philip." We are to conclude that he was there one moment and gone the next, to the eunuch's amazement. The same will be true of us, but to the world's

---

2. Gr. HARPAZO, Acts 8:39; John 6:15; II Cor. 12:4; Acts 23:10.

amazement. "When Jesus therefore perceived that they would come and *take Him by force,* to make Him a King, He departed again into a mountain Himself alone." In like fashion, we are going to be removed from the earth with such force that neither men nor angels will be able to hinder our departure in any way. Such a demonstration of God's power will probably cause all heaven to break forth in a song of deliverance! The Apostle Paul as we know was "caught up into paradise." In other words, he was transported from one location to another. Like Paul, some day soon we too are going to be translated to heaven, which is our eternal home. Our phrase is also associated with being rescued from danger. "The chief captain, fearing lest Paul should have been pulled in pieces of them, commanded the soldiers to go down, and to *take him by force* from among them. . . ." There is reason to believe that the true Church is going to face another blood bath as we approach the time of the Rapture. This will come, of course, at the hands of godless men who resist the truth of God. In all likelihood, just as this final persecution is escalating the Church will be rescued from its adversaries (II Tim. 3:11,12).

For the present, members of His Body are separated due to death, doctrinal differences, geographical distance, etc. But in that day we shall be "caught up *together* with them in the clouds." Family reunions are interesting times to say the least. They give us the opportunity to visit with family and friends, many of whom we haven't seen for years. We reminisce about the good old days and marvel at how everyone has grown older since the last time we saw them—ourselves excluded! Usually there is one older family patriarch whom everyone looks forward to visiting with. Their presence seems to bring back memories of our Godly heritage.

Similarly, the whole family of heaven will be *captivated* by our Savior who washed us in His own precious blood. Furthermore, we are going to see those who were once so dear to us, not to mention the Apostle Paul who will undoubtedly claim a lot of attention.

4. THE JUDGMENT SEAT OF CHRIST

". . . to meet the Lord in the air: and so shall we ever be with the Lord" (I Thes. 4:17).

Upon our arrival in heaven we must *all* appear before the Judgment Seat of Christ. Since we were *stewards of the mysteries* of God this judgment will primarily take into account the *conduct* of every member of the Body of Christ. There are three basic areas that are going to be reviewed as we stand before the Lord at the *Bema Seat*. First and foremost, did we acquire a well-rounded knowledge of Paul's gospel? Secondly, were we faithful in making the *Mystery* known and did we apply the grace of God to our lives that we might walk well pleasing unto Him who called us? Thirdly, were we careful to proclaim the whole counsel of God in light of Paul's revelation?

The outcome of this examination should be of particular interest to every believer, especially in view of the eternal ramifications. Our actions *now* will either pay dividends or cause us to suffer loss in eternity. For example, one's *faithfulness* to the message of grace will have a bearing on his reigning position with Christ (II Tim. 2:11-13). In addition, the degree that the believer's body will be glorified is determined by his or her *stand* for the gospel of the grace of God (I Cor. 15:39-42). Finally, the rewards that each believer is promised are based on how *faithfully* he dispensed the revelation of the Mystery. Of course, those who never had any

Our Blessed Hope

exposure to the Mystery will only be held accountable for the light they had. God ". . . will make manifest the counsels of the hearts: and then shall every man have praise of God." (I Cor. 4:5).

For those who have been remiss in standing in the defense of Paul's gospel, please heed these words: *For we must all appear before the Judgment Seat of Christ; that every one may receive the things done in His Body, according to that he hath done, whether it be good or bad [of no value]"* (II Cor. 5:10).

THE OBJECTIVE OF THE RAPTURE

The objective then of the *Secret Coming of Christ* is to catch the Church away to glory that we might escape the wrath of God to come. Following the Judgment Seat of Christ every member of the Body of Christ will be seated with Christ in the heavenlies far above all principalities and powers. Here we will reign with Christ in a position of *exaltation* for all eternity. It is a wonder of God's grace when we pause to consider that we have been saved by grace, given a heavenly hope and calling, granted eternal life, and blessed with all spiritual blessings, but there is more, much more!

> "And hath raised us up together, and made us sit together in heavenly places in Christ Jesus: that in the ages to come He might show the exceeding riches of His grace toward us through Christ Jesus " (Eph. 2:6,7).

After all God has bestowed upon us He is going to show His *kindness* toward us in the ages to come—phenomenal! We will behold the beauty, splendor and vastness of the heavenly realm, which is our inheritance. Myriads of angels will be at our beck and call. The Church the Body of Christ has the highest calling of all of the other saints of God in other ages. The basis for this favor is "we walk by faith and not by sight," whereas, the saints in other ages walked by faith and by sight. What a future we have as members of His Body! Indeed, we do have a BLESSED HOPE.

15

Practical Instructions for Living Under Grace

> "If ye then be risen with Christ, seek those things which are above, where Christ sitteth on the right hand of God. Set your affection on things above, not on things on the earth."
> —*Colossians 3:1,2*

With most things in life instruction precedes practice. Instruction normally begins with general information followed by safety tips for proper operation. Once this is accomplished we put into practice what we have learned.

I remember vividly when I was learning to drive that my driving instructor literally spent hours explaining the function of every pedal, knob and lever. He spent one entire session elaborating on the proper use of the hand or emergency brake. The instructor pointed out that most drivers would have to use the hand brake in an *emergency* probably only once or twice in their entire driving career. He went on to add that there were two things I must never forget about that hand brake: One, don't panic, think to use it in the event of an emergency; secondly, apply it slowly so as not to lock the brakes and throw the car out of control. Little did I realize at the time that I would have to put that counsel into practice so soon.

Two years later I was driving to the *Carnegie Museum* in Pittsburgh, where I worked, when I had one of the most frightening experiences of my life. As I drove down through town I went to apply the foot brake to stop at an upcoming traffic light, only to find that the pedal went straight to the floor! Talk about a helpless feeling, that was it! I looked down in unbelief and when I looked back up again I was heading straight for the back of a brand new Cadillac! Unable to swerve due to traffic I quickly, though gradually, applied the emergency brake bringing the old 1956 Plymouth to a stop within a gnat's eyelash of the Cadillac's bumper. Those who were with me that day lived to tell the story, though they aged a few years in the process.

In our spiritual lives the principle of instruction preceding practice is also true. As with life in general, instruction that is not applied or that is unheeded is of little value. God would have us put to use in every day Christian experience what He has imparted to us from His Word. It is one thing to know the Word of truth, but it is an entirely different matter to make an *application* of it in our lives. We might fully understand that we are to "love our neighbor," but if we do not come to our neighbor's aid in a time of need of what profit is our knowledge? This is why the Apostle Paul challenges us to *seek* and *set*.

SEEKING THINGS ABOVE

"If ye then be risen with Christ, seek those things which are above, where Christ sitteth on the right hand of God" (Col. 3:1).

When Paul writes to the Colossians, "If ye then be risen with Christ," he is not questioning their salvation as some have supposed. The term "if" in the Scriptures can be used in two senses. First, it can be used in the suppositional sense when a thing is supposed, such as in a hypothetical case. For example, I might say, *"If* I were the President of the United States I would abolish abortion!" The word "if" can also be used in a challenging sense to emphasize a particular fact. You might say to your son, *"If* you're 21 then why don't you act like it?" This is precisely how the Apostle Paul uses the "if" in the above passage when he addresses the Colossians. He is challenging them with the fact that since they are risen with Christ they should be seeking and setting their affections on things above.

But what exactly does Paul mean by the words, "seek those things which are above?" We believe he is encouraging the Colossians, and us, to *seek out* the blessings we have received as members of the Body of Christ—that is, to seek out what they are. This gives the writer one last opportunity to show the importance of rightly dividing the Word of truth.

Envision yourself living back in the days of Moses, and let's suppose that you were a newcomer to the camp of Israel. Having just come to God you inquire of Moses, What blessings will we receive if we render obedience to the Law? Without a moment's hesitation Moses would have stroked his beard and replied, God has promised us a land (on the earth) that is flowing with milk and honey. And if His people (Israel) will honor His name and keep His statutes He will bless the fruit of the womb and fill the Promised Land. Our cattle will be greatly multiplied and will stand on a thousand hills. The bread basket on the

Hebrew table will always be filled in addition to the storehouses overflowing. Should any enemy endanger our borders the Lord shall smite them and cause them to flee in seven directions (Deut. 28:3-8).

Moving from the dispensation of the Law to the dispensation of Grace there is a change in emphasis on the blessings enjoyed. When we *seek* out what our blessings are in the administration of Grace we learn that we have been blessed with all *spiritual blessings* in heavenly places. Had you had the privilege of sitting down by the campfire with the Apostle Paul he would not have hesitated to inform you that as members of the Body of Christ you have a *heavenly* hope and calling. Paul would not have rested until you understood that you are: Chosen in Christ Jesus; adopted; accepted in the Beloved; washed in the blood, forgiven of your sins; given to know the Mystery of His will; sealed with the Holy Spirit; and receiving an inheritance with the saints in light (Eph. 1:3-14).

The foregoing chapters are but a sampling of the spiritual blessings we enjoy in Christ. May the Lord guide us in discovering the others that are found in the Pauline epistles. After we determine what our blessings are, then we are to *set* our affection on things above.

SETTING OUR AFFECTION ON THINGS ABOVE

"Set your affection on things above, not on things on the earth" (Col. 3:2).

Here is where practice comes into the picture. Setting our *affection* on our spiritual blessings means that we should fill our *hearts* with them to the point that we desire to know everything there is to know about each and every blessing. Eventually this should permeate our everyday Christian experience resulting in a change in our conduct. To show you what we mean, let us take the spiritual blessing of *being accepted in the Beloved* and meditate on it for a few moments.

We often hear people refer to accepting Christ as their personal Savior and, of course, we understand what they mean and rejoice with them in their salvation. But to be more precise we are not asked to *accept,* but rather to *believe.* You will remember that God said to Cain that if he brought the proper sacrifice he would be accepted. Cain's responsibility was to *believe* what God had said and bring the sacrificial lamb; it was God who would do the accepting (Gen. 4:3-7). The Israelites, when carrying out the steps of the Levitical offerings were careful to bring the offering to the door of the Tabernacle *before* the Lord, that it might be *accepted* of the Lord for the atonement of their sins (Lev. 4:3,4). When God the Father looked down from heaven and saw His dear Son drenched in blood, He *accepted* the once for all sacrifice of His Son as the provision for our salvation. The work has been accomplished on our behalf; now it is given unto us to *believe,* at which time we are *accepted by God* in the Beloved One, having full access into the heavenlies (Eph. 1:6; Phil. 1:29; Heb.10:19,20).

A small boy asked a preacher: "Sir, what can I do to be saved?" The preacher replied. "Son, you're too late." "What!" exclaimed the boy, "too late to be saved?" "No," said the preacher, "too late to do anything. You see, son, Jesus already did it all two thousand years ago." Christ's death is adequate. He paid our full debt of sin, leaving nothing for us to do or pay! This is actually what Acts 16:31 teaches: There's nothing to do; just *believe* on the Lord Jesus Christ and thou shalt be saved.

When we fill our minds with the wonderful truth that we have been *accepted in the Beloved,* what more can we do but *surrender* ourselves to the One who first loved us? After we come to know Christ as our personal Savior the things of this world that were once so important now seem insignificant. Now the purpose of our heart is (or should be) to present our bodies a living sacrifice, holy, *acceptable unto God,* which is our reasonable service (Rom. 12:1,2). While there are literally millions of things in this world to occupy our minds, may God help us to follow in the footsteps of the apostle *to seek and set* our affection on the things which are above, where Christ sitteth on the right hand of God Almighty.

"Finally, brethren, whatsoever things are true, whatsoever things are honest, whatsoever things are just, whatsoever things are pure, whatsoever things are lovely, whatsoever things are of good report; if there be any virtue, and if there be any praise, THINK ON THESE THINGS"—Philippians 4:8,9.

Scripture Index

Genesis

Reference	Page
1-3	52
1:1	25
1:7	16
1:9,10	16
1:14	17
1:26,27	55
1:27	130
1:27,28	54
1:28	55
2:5,8,9	55
2:16,17	55
2:20	129
3:6	55
3:7	54,55
3:14-19,23,24	55
3:22	56
4-11	52
4:1-4	56
4:3-7	177
4:5-15	56
4:16-24	56
4:19	56
6:13	56
6:17	56
7:1,7,16	100
9:1-7	54
9:2	56
9:3	56
9:5,6	56
9:6	57
9:7	57
11:3,4	57
11:4	57
11:7-9	57
12	52
12:1-3	34,54
12:2	58
12:3	58

Genesis (Cont'd)

Reference	Page
13:14-17	54
15:17,18	58
17:9-14	58
25:24-34	58
26:1-4	58
26:1-6	58
28:10-15	58
41:54-57	58
46:26	58

Exodus

1:7-22	59
19,20	54
19-23	18
19:3-7	59
19:5	18,24
19:5,6	18
19:6	147
19:8	59
20	59
21	59
24	19
24:6-8	18
29:1,4	146
31:12-17	25
32:1-6	60
32:27,28	140
35:3	25

Leviticus

4:1-7	20
4:3,4	177
10:1-3	140
16	59
23:1-10	110

Numbers

10:1-10	166
12:1-10	140

179

Numbers (Cont'd)

Reference	Page
13:26-33	60
16:1-8	60
25:1-3	60

Deuteronomy

28:3-8	176

Joshua

7:25,26	140

I Samuel

13:8-14	29

II Samuel

7:16	63
7:16,17	31

II Kings

17:4-6,15-18	60

II Chronicles

5:12-14	166
36:11-21	60

Job

19:25,26	29,34

Psalms

2:1-5	166
2:1-12	54,62,122
7:6	46
19:1-4	138
103:8-12	87
104:5	64,69

Proverbs

16:33	39

Isaiah

9:6,7	63
24:1	62

Isaiah (Cont'd)

Reference	Page
35:1-6	30
52:15	148
61:1,2	16
65:17	64
65:20	63

Jeremiah

23:5	28
23:5,6	63
30:7	62
31:31	23,24
31:32	60
31:33	23
38:6	114

Ezekiel

36:25	148
36:26,27	23
38:14-23	62

Daniel

4:35	38,157

Zephaniah

1:14-18	122

Zechariah

13:6-9	122
14:4	89

Matthew

1	21
5:5	30,34
5:17	19
6:10	30
8:1-4	84
8:3,4	20
10:5,6	34
10:5-7	78
12:31,32	46

Scripture Index

Matthew (Cont'd)

Reference	Page
13:11	78
13:24-30	78
13:36-43	78
15:22	94,95
15:22-24	93
15:24	34,95
15:27,28	95
15:28	95
16:28	28,34
17:1-5	34
19:28	40,63
23:1-3	20,83
24:3,14	53
24:4-31	78
24:20	63
24:27-31	88
24:29,30	62
24:30	89
25:1-13	88
25:14-30	64
25:14-46	89
25:31-46	64
26:17-28	23
26:28	23
27:51-53	166
28:20	84

Mark

Reference	Page
1:4,5	148,150
1:8	109
16:15,16	63
16:16	147,150

Luke

Reference	Page
1:67-70	34
1:67-77	23
1:68-70	31

Luke (Cont'd)

Reference	Page
4:16-20	16
4:21	16
7:28-30	147
7:29,30	78
12:35-40	88
12:50	101
16:16	38
19:11,12	30
22:19,20	21

John

Reference	Page
1:11	48
1:31	148
1:49	38
5:28,29	166
6:15	168
8:42-44	155
11:25	124
12:20-23	94
14	107
14:16	106
14:17	108
14:26	107
19:31-33	23
20:22	38
20:31	150

Acts

Reference	Page
1	38
1:3	38
1:4	88
1:5	109
1:8	109
1:21,22	38
1:23	37,39
1:24	39
1:26	39
2	76,109
2:1,4	109

Acts (Cont'd)

Reference	Page
2:1-10	114
2:4	110,112
2:14	39
2:17-21	88
2:19,20	68
2:38	63
2:44,45	110
3:14-21	110
3:19,21	31
3:21	34
4:32-37	110
6:2	39
6:5	45
6:8	44
6:13,14	45
6:15	45
7	31,45,60
7:2	44
7:51	46
7:56	46
8	52
8:39	168
9	39,53
9,22,26	35
13:15,16	47
13:42	48
13:46	49
15:10	59
16:20-25	114
16:31	178
17:11	16
18:6	49
20:24	47,81
23:10	168
26:9-12	43
26:13-15	43
26:16	41,42,85
26:16,17	47

Acts (Cont'd)

Reference	Page
26:16-19	43
26:19	37
28:27,28	50

Romans

Reference	Page
1	57
1:16	47
1:21	137
1:22,23	57
1:24,26,28	138
2:5,6	141
2:14,15	54,56
3:19,20	18
3:20	59
3:21,25	101
3:25	149
4:5	75,151
5:6-11	75
6:3,4	111,151
6:14	21,61
6:14,15	84
11:7-12,15,30	139
11:7,20,26-32	148
11:11	46
11:13	35,42,47,74
11:15	47
11:31,32	85
12:1,2	61,178
14:10	62
14:10-12	87
15:8	82,83
15:27	24
16:7	98,99
16:25	33,34,36,61,77,81,87

I Corinthians

Reference	Page
1:1	74
1:14-17	149
1:17	149

Scripture Index

I Corinthians (Cont'd)

Reference	Page
2:8	134
2:10-12	107
3:9-15	27
3:9-17	62
4:5	171
5:7	23
6:19	160
9:1	41
9:2	41
9:16-18	61
10:1-15	62
10:11	52
11:1	124
11:3	131
11:23	22
11:32	128
12	104
12:11	108
12:12,13	75
12:13	61,74,103,111
12:13,27	152
12:14,15	104
12:18	104
12:27	34,103
13:10	151
14:33	145
14:37	9,41,86,132
15:1-4	103
15:3,4	75
15:7	39
15:19,20	123
15:27,28	65
15:39-42	170
15:51	87
15:51,52	168

II Corinthians

3:6	24
4:17	92

II Corinthians (Cont'd)

Reference	Page
5:2	124
5:4	123
5:8	123,164
5:9	65
5:10	67,171
5:10,11	62
5:14,15	143
5:14,15,16	97
5:14-20	75
5:17	60,74,96,97
5:18	137
5:19	140
5:20	122,141
6:9	128
12:1	44
12:4	168
12:7-10	160
12:12	41

Galatians

1:1	36
1:4	53
1:11,12	41,77
1:16,17	43
2:7	81
2:20	152
4:4,5	19
5:16-26	61
6:1	105

Ephesians

1:1,3	102
1:3,11	69
1:3-14	176
1:4,5	156
1:6	177
1:7	149
1:10	54,64,65
1:11	66

183

Ephesians (Cont'd)

Reference	Page
1:13-15	75
1:19-23	32,34
1:20,21	133,148
1:20-23	43,60,74,86
1:22,23	34,60
2:2	156
2:4-7	75
2:6	32,33,34,98
2:6,7	64,69,171
2:7	53
2:8,9	75,151
2:11,12	94
2:11-16	74
2:13	96
2:14-17	60
3:1-3	31,36,72
3:1-4	34
3:1-6	54
3:1,7,8	74
3:2	60
3:2,3	53
3:2,9	77
3:3	81
3:5	33,76,77
3:8	73,81
3:9	61
3:10,11	69
4:3,4	106
4:3-6	91
4:4	92,117,119,120
4:4-6	40
4:5	61,75,111,127,136,144,152
4:6	154,155,156,157,160
4:30	107
5:18	111
5:19-21	114
5:23,24	74,128
5:26,27	132

Philippians

Reference	Page
1:6	122
1:21	125
1:23	125
1:29	177
2:9	60
2:27	159
3:20	33,34,125
4:8,9	178

Colossians

1:5	33,34,43
1:18	43,60,74,97
1:21-23	75
1:24-26	99
1:25	79,151
1:25,26	51,80
1:25-27	34
1:26	33,37
1:27	160
2:11	150,152
2:12,13	152
2:14	21,22,150,151
2:14-17	61
2:15	133
3:1	174
3:1,2	173
3:1-4	34
3:2	176

I Thessalonians

1:3	120
1:10	61,87,123
4	88
4:13	164
4:13-18	61,75,87,103
4:14	165,167
4:15,16	124
4:16	165
4:16,17	87

Scripture Index

I Thessalonians (Cont'd)
Reference	Page
4:17	87,166,170
5	121
5:5	121,122
5:8	121
5:9	123

I Timothy
1:1	120
1:11	81
1:12-16	99
1:15,16	43,103
1:16	124
2:3-7	21
2:5-7	102

II Timothy
1:15	9,51,61
2:8	81
2:11-13	170
2:15	15,83
3:11,12	169
4:5	61
4:7	81

Titus
1:2	119,136
2:13	61,75,163
3:5	151

Hebrews
6:19	119
9:1	146
9:10	146
9:14	102
10:9,10	24
10:19,20	177
11:4	56
11:10	30
12:6-10	128

Hebrews (Cont'd)
Reference	Page
13	53

James
1	53

I Peter
2:7,8	148
3:20,21	101
3:21	101

II Peter
1:15-21	34
1:16,17,19	27
3:10	64
3:11,12	64
3:12,13	68

Jude
14	88

Revelation
1:7	89
7:1-8	62
9:21	63
11:15	62
11:15-19	54
12:7-9	67
16:11,21	63
20	53,54
20:4,5,7	62
20:7-9	63
20:11-15	64
21,22	53
21:1	64
21:4	65
21:9-21	69
21:9-27	64
21:14	40
22:1-5	69

CASSETTE TAPE RECORDINGS FOR FURTHERING YOUR UNDERSTANDING OF THE WORD, RIGHTLY DIVIDED BY PASTOR PAUL M. SADLER

1. *Heaven:* This album contains four-cassette tapes which describe the glories of the heavenlies.

2. *Prayer, Dispensationally Considered:* This three-cassette album focuses on the prayer life of the believer in the present administration of Grace.

3. *Pretribulational Rapture of the Church:* This album contains four-cassette tapes that are designed to help the child of God prepare for coming events.

4. *Understanding Dispensationalism:* This six-cassette album presents all of the dispensations in clear, understandable language.

5. *Hard Sayings of St. Paul:* This two-cassette album deals with some of the more difficult passages found in Paul's epistles.

6. *Dispensational Position of John's Writings:* This eight-cassette album primarily focuses on where the writings of the Apostle John fit into the overall scheme of things.

7. *Revelation, A Dispensational Introduction:* This album contains three-cassette tapes that are devoted to clearing up the confusion that often surrounds the early chapters of the Book of Revelation.

For a *free* Tape Catalog, simply write to: The *Berean Bible Society,* N112 W17761 Mequon Rd., Germantown, Wisconsin 53022.

THE BEREAN SEARCHLIGHT

YOU CAN HELP GET THIS MESSAGE OUT TO OTHERS

*Send for our free Bible Study Magazine
and a full Price List of our Literature*

BEREAN BIBLE SOCIETY
N112 W17761 Mequon Rd.
Germantown, Wisconsin 53022
(Metro Milwaukee)

THE BEREAN BIBLE SOCIETY

For over 50 years the *Berean Bible Society* has been "An Organization for the Promotion of Bible Study." Standing firm on the fundamentals of the Christian faith, it employs many means to interest people in the study of the Scriptures, among them the following:

BBS arranges *Bible Conferences* for the study of the Word. Its President, Paul Sadler, has spoken at many such conferences throughout the United States and Canada.

The Society publishes the *Berean Searchlight,* a Bible study magazine edited by Pastor Sadler, and sent free of charge to readers in every state in the Union and more than 60 foreign countries.

"Two Minutes With the Bible," a weekly newspaper column featured in hundreds of newspapers across the country, is another means BBS uses to reach the masses with the Word. This column now has a weekly readership running into the millions.

Tape recorded messages are provided free of charge through our free lending library and for use in Bible classes. Some taped messages are offered for sale at modest prices.

BBS has been proclaiming the message of grace for many years through *radio broadcasts* in many parts of the country.

These growing ministries are carried on by the voluntary contributions of believers who desire to see others reached with the truths that have brought so much light and blessing to their own lives.

The Triumph of His Grace
Preparing Ourselves For the Rapture

By

Paul M. Sadler

This volume is a comprehensive study on the doctrine of the Pretribulational Rapture of the Church. Midtribulationism, Pre-wrath, Posttribulationism and the Partial Rapture theories are thoroughly examined under the microscope of the Word, rightly divided. *The Triumph of His Grace* also contains *charts, outlines, time lines* and *numerous comparisons* to help the reader understand that the Body of Christ will be "delivered from the wrath to come."

225 PAGES

(Includes Scripture Index)

CLOTHBOUND   GOLD STAMPED

ORDER YOUR COPY TODAY!

BEREAN BIBLE SOCIETY

N112 W17761 Mequon Rd.   Germantown, WI 53022

(Metro Milwaukee)

NOTES

P 99
P 103 Church Started at the Conversion of Paul (With the Age of Grace).